The Static Beneath the Skin

The Static Beneath the Skin

Suzanne Byrd

CONTENTS

1

Introduction: The Crash

Imagine waking up one morning and realizing you can't do it anymore. The emails pile up, the to-do list feels insurmountable, and even the simplest tasks—like showering or making breakfast—feel like climbing a mountain. You've been here before, but this time is different. This time, it's not just exhaustion or stress; it's a complete shutdown. Your body feels heavy, your mind is foggy, and the thought of 'pushing through' makes you want to cry. If this sounds familiar, you're not alone. This is what neurodivergent burnout feels like, and it's a crisis that demands a different kind of solution.

Neurodivergent burnout is not your typical burnout. It's not just about working too hard or needing a vacation. It's a neurological collapse that happens when your brain reaches its breaking point after years of suppressing who you are to fit into a world that wasn't designed for you. This chapter will explore what neurodivergent burnout is, why it happens, and why traditional burnout remedies often make things worse. By the end, you'll have a clearer understanding of your experience and the first steps toward reclaiming your energy and sense of self.

The Wall at 35: The Math of Masking

For many women, burnout hits hardest in their mid-thirties. This isn't a coincidence—it's the culmination of decades of masking. Masking is the practice of hiding your natural neurodivergent behaviors to fit societal norms. It's forcing eye contact when it feels uncomfortable, scripting conversations to avoid awkward pauses, or suppressing stims like fidgeting or rocking. On the surface, masking helps you blend in and succeed. But underneath, it's exhausting. Every act of masking is a withdrawal from your sensory and cognitive reserves, and eventually, those reserves run dry.

Think of it like a credit card: every time you mask, you're borrowing from your energy account. For years, you might keep up with the payments, but the debt keeps growing. By your mid-thirties, the compounding interest of sensory overload, emotional suppression, and cognitive overextension catches up with you. Suddenly, what used to feel manageable—your job, your relationships, even your daily routines—feels impossible. This is what I call 'the math of masking,' and it's why so many neurodivergent women hit a wall at this stage of life.

Neurodivergent Burnout vs. Corporate Burnout

Neurodivergent burnout is often mistaken for corporate burnout, but the two are fundamentally different. Corporate burnout is typically caused by external factors like overwork, lack of support, or toxic workplace environments. The usual advice—take a vacation, practice mindfulness, or socialize more—might help someone with corporate burnout, but for neurodivergent individuals, these solutions can be actively harmful.

Take Jane, for example. A successful marketing executive, Jane was diagnosed with ADHD at 32. After years of pushing herself to meet deadlines and socialize with colleagues, she hit a breaking point. Her therapist suggested she join a book club to 'recharge her social battery.' But instead of feeling rejuvenated, Jane felt even more drained. What she needed wasn't more social interaction—it was quiet, unstructured time to recover from the sensory overload of her daily life.

This is a common experience for neurodivergent individuals. Our burnout isn't just about stress; it's about sensory and cognitive overwhelm. Treating it like corporate burnout can exacerbate the problem, leaving us feeling misunderstood and defeated.

You're Not Broken: Misaligned Voltage

One of the hardest parts of neurodivergent burnout is the shame and self-blame that often accompany it. You might feel like you're failing at life, like everyone else has it together while you're falling apart. But here's the truth: you're not broken. Your burnout is a natural response to living in a world that doesn't match your neurological 'voltage.'

Imagine trying to power a high-voltage appliance with a low-voltage outlet. No matter how hard you try, the appliance won't work properly—and eventually, it will burn out. The same principle applies to neurodivergent brains. When we're forced to operate in environments that don't align with our neurological needs, our systems overload, and burnout becomes inevitable.

The good news is that small adjustments can make a big difference. Reducing sensory input, creating a low-demand environment, and allowing yourself to unmask can help you regain your energy and focus. It's not about fixing yourself—it's about creating conditions that allow you to thrive.

The High-Masking Trap: Dissociation and Delayed Processing

High masking doesn't just drain your energy; it disconnects you from yourself. Many neurodivergent women describe feeling like they're 'on autopilot,' going through the motions of life without really being present. This is dissociation, and it's a common coping mechanism for dealing with sensory and emotional overwhelm.

Dissociation can also lead to delayed processing. You might not realize how exhausted or overwhelmed you are until weeks or even months after the fact. This makes it especially hard to recognize burnout before it becomes severe. By the time you realize something is wrong, you're already in crisis mode.

Consider Sarah, a teacher diagnosed with Autism at 38. For years, she managed her demanding job by suppressing her sensory sensitivities and scripting her interactions with students and colleagues. She appeared successful and put-together, but inside, she was barely holding on. It wasn't until she completely broke down—unable to get out of bed for days—that she realized how burnt out she was. Recognizing the early warning signs of burnout—like chronic fatigue, sensory overload, or emotional numbness—can help you intervene before it's too late.

Why Traditional Burnout Solutions Fail

Traditional burnout solutions often fail neurodivergent individuals because they don't address the root cause of the problem. Cognitive Behavioral Therapy (CBT), for example, focuses on changing negative thought patterns. But for neurodivergent people, burnout isn't just about thoughts—it's about sensory overload, social exhaustion, and neurological mismatches. When CBT tells you to 'think positively' about situations that are inherently overwhelming, it can feel invalidating or even gaslighting.

Similarly, mindfulness and exercise—common recommendations for burnout—can backfire if not tailored to neurodivergent needs. Mindfulness can be overwhelming for individuals with sensory sensitivities, while intense exercise can exacerbate physical fatigue. Instead of blindly following generic advice, it's important to find strategies that work for your unique brain and body.

Setting the Stage for Recovery

Recovering from neurodivergent burnout requires a different approach—one that prioritizes sensory regulation, energy conservation, and strategic unmasking. This book will guide you through the process of creating a low-demand lifestyle that aligns with your neurological needs. You'll learn how to identify and honor your sensory limits, reduce unnecessary cognitive loads, and gradually unmask in ways that feel safe and empowering.

The journey isn't about becoming 'normal' or 'fixing' yourself. It's about reclaiming your authentic self and finding ways to thrive in a world that wasn't designed for you. As you move through the chapters, you'll discover how to create an environment that supports rather than drains you, how to build a toolkit of sensory-first strategies, and how to advocate for your needs in a way that feels sustainable.

By the end of this book, you'll have the tools and understanding to move from survival to thriving—not by pushing through, but by aligning your life with your true self. Welcome to the beginning of your unmasking journey. Let's take the first step together.

2

Defining Neurodivergent Burnout

Burnout is a term we hear often in our high-demand world, but not all burnout is created equal. For neurodivergent individuals—particularly those with ADHD or Autism—burnout is not simply the result of overwork or prolonged stress. It is a distinct, neurologically rooted condition that arises from years of suppressing natural behaviors, masking to fit societal expectations, and enduring sensory overload. This chapter aims to define Neurodivergent Burnout, distinguish it from the more commonly discussed Corporate Burnout, and illuminate why traditional approaches to recovery often fail—or even harm—those experiencing it.

Neurodivergent Burnout vs. Corporate Burnout

Corporate Burnout is typically described as a state of physical and emotional exhaustion caused by prolonged workplace stress. It often manifests as feelings of detachment, reduced performance, and cynicism toward one's job. While this form of burnout is undeniably challenging, it is fundamentally different from Neurodivergent Burnout.

Neurodivergent Burnout, on the other hand, is rooted in the neurological processes of ADHD and Autism. It occurs when the brain's ability to process information becomes overwhelmed due to years of masking—a term that refers to the conscious or unconscious suppression of neurodivergent traits to appear "normal." Masking can include behaviors like forcing oneself to make eye contact, suppressing stimming (self-stimulating behaviors), or mimicking social cues to fit in. While this may help neurodivergent individuals navigate a neurotypical world, it comes at a significant cost: chronic fatigue, sensory overload, and a loss of executive function.

Standard burnout recovery strategies often exacerbate Neurodivergent Burnout. For example, encouraging someone to "socialize more" or "push through" can be deeply harmful. Socializing may require masking, which further depletes energy reserves. Pushing through ignores the neurological limitations of the brain, leading to even greater exhaustion. Understanding these distinctions is crucial for developing effective recovery strategies tailored to neurodivergent needs.

Symptoms and Signs of Neurodivergent Burnout

Neurodivergent Burnout manifests in ways that are distinct from Corporate Burnout. Common symptoms include chronic fatigue, sensory overload, loss of executive function, and emotional dysregulation. Each of these symptoms reflects the brain's struggle to cope with prolonged stress and suppression of natural behaviors.

Chronic fatigue in Neurodivergent Burnout is not just physical tiredness but a profound exhaustion that permeates every aspect of life. It is the result of the brain constantly working overtime to process sensory input, navigate social interactions, and suppress neurodivergent traits.

Sensory overload is another hallmark. For neurodivergent individuals, everyday stimuli—such as bright lights, loud noises, or crowded spaces—can feel overwhelming. In a state of burnout, the brain's ability to filter and process these stimuli is compromised, making even minor sensory input unbearable.

Loss of executive function is particularly debilitating. Executive function refers to cognitive processes like planning, organizing, and prioritizing. In Neurodivergent Burnout, these abilities deteriorate, making it difficult to complete even simple tasks. This can lead to feelings of helplessness and frustration, further exacerbating the burnout cycle.

Emotional dysregulation is also common. Neurodivergent individuals may experience heightened emotional responses or difficulty managing their emotions. This can manifest as sudden outbursts, intense anxiety, or a sense of emotional numbness.

Consider the case of Emma, a 35-year-old woman recently diagnosed with Autism. For years, Emma excelled in her corporate job, masking her need for routine and sensory breaks to appear "professional." Over time, she began experiencing chronic fatigue, headaches, and an inability to focus. Despite her best efforts, she could no longer keep up with the demands of her job. Her doctor diagnosed her with Chronic Fatigue Syndrome, but traditional treatments provided little relief. It wasn't until she learned about Neurodivergent Burnout that Emma understood the root cause of her struggles: her brain had reached its limit after years of masking and sensory overload.

Why Misdiagnosis is Common

Neurodivergent Burnout is frequently misdiagnosed, often confused with conditions like Chronic Fatigue Syndrome, Fibromyalgia, or Generalized Anxiety Disorder. This misdiagnosis stems from several factors, including societal biases, a lack of awareness among medical professionals, and the challenges faced by high-masking individuals in articulating their experiences.

Society often dismisses neurodivergent traits as personality quirks or moral failings rather than neurological differences. This bias can lead doctors to overlook the underlying causes of symptoms, attributing them to mental health conditions like depression or anxiety. For example, emotional dysregulation may be labeled as "overreacting," while sensory overload may be dismissed as "being too sensitive."

High-masking individuals face additional challenges in receiving accurate diagnoses. Because they have learned to suppress their neurodivergent traits, their struggles may not align with stereotypical presentations of ADHD or Autism. They may appear outwardly successful, masking their internal exhaustion and overwhelm. This can lead to dismissive responses like, "You're doing fine—what's the problem?"

Consider Sarah, a 40-year-old woman with ADHD who thrived in her career as a teacher. Despite her achievements, she struggled with chronic fatigue, memory lapses, and anxiety. Her therapist recommended Cognitive Behavioral Therapy (CBT), but Sarah found it ineffective—her struggles were neurological, not just "negative thoughts." It wasn't until she discovered Neurodivergent Burnout that she realized her symptoms were the result of years of masking her ADHD traits and overextending herself in a high-demand profession.

Neurodivergent Burnout is a distinct condition that requires a nuanced understanding and tailored approach to recovery. Unlike Corporate Burnout, it is rooted in the neurological processes of ADHD and Autism, exacerbated by years of masking and sensory overload. Recognizing the symptoms—chronic fatigue, sensory overload, loss of executive function, and emotional dysregulation—is the first step toward healing. Misdiagnosis is common due to societal biases and a lack of awareness, but with greater understanding, neurodivergent individuals can find the support they need.

By acknowledging the unique challenges of Neurodivergent Burnout, we can move beyond traditional, often harmful recovery strategies and develop approaches that honor the brain's limitations and needs. In the following chapters, we will explore practical steps for recovery, from embracing self-compassion to creating sensory-friendly environments. The journey to reclaiming your neurodivergent brain begins with understanding—and this chapter is your first step.

3

The Physiology of Masking

For many women who receive a late diagnosis of ADHD or Autism, the realization often comes with a mix of relief and grief. Relief, because it finally explains a lifetime of feeling "different," and grief, because it uncovers the toll that years of masking has taken on their bodies and minds. Masking, the act of suppressing natural neurodivergent behaviors to fit societal norms, is often second nature to those who have spent years trying to "pass" as neurotypical. But what happens when the cost of "looking normal" catches up with you?

This chapter explores the physiological and neurological consequences of masking, shedding light on why so many high-masking individuals experience chronic fatigue, sensory overwhelm, and burnout. By understanding the mechanisms behind these symptoms, you can begin to reclaim your body and mind, moving toward a more authentic and sustainable way of living.

The Cost of 'Looking Normal'

Masking behaviors—such as suppressing stims, forcing eye contact, or scripting conversations—may seem like small adjustments, but they come at a significant biological cost. These actions require constant cognitive effort, activating the body's stress response and flooding the system with cortisol. Over time, this chronic stress can lead to a cascade of physical symptoms, including chronic fatigue, fibromyalgia-like pain, and other "mystery illnesses" that defy easy diagnosis.

Take stimming, for example. For many neurodivergent individuals, repetitive movements like rocking, hand-flapping, or tapping are a natural way to self-regulate emotions and sensory input. Suppressing these behaviors forces the body to hold onto that energy, creating a kind of internal pressure that can manifest as tension headaches, muscle pain, or even gastrointestinal issues.

Similarly, forcing eye contact during conversations can feel like trying to hold a weighty gaze for hours on end. The effort it takes to maintain this socially expected behavior can leave you feeling drained and disconnected, as though you've just run a marathon in your mind.

The first step toward mitigating these costs is recognizing the behaviors you've been suppressing and understanding their purpose. Are you biting your tongue instead of speaking your mind? Clenching your fists instead of fidgeting? These small acts of self-denial add up, and addressing them requires intentionality. Start by identifying safe spaces where you can let your guard down, even if it's just for a few minutes a day. Allow yourself to stim, to look away, to speak freely. These moments of authenticity, however brief, can begin to ease the strain on your body.

The Chameleon Effect: Dissociation and Delayed Processing

For high-masking individuals, survival often means slipping into a kind of chameleon mode—blending into the environment by dissociating from your own body and emotions. This "chameleon effect" allows you to navigate high-demand situations, but it comes at a profound cost.

Dissociation can make it difficult to recognize your own feelings in the moment. You might find yourself going through the motions of a conversation or task only to realize hours or even days later that you were deeply upset, angry, or exhausted. This delayed emotional processing can create a disconnect between your mind and body, leaving you feeling untethered and out of sync with yourself.

Consider Sarah, a 35-year-old marketing executive who often found herself nodding along in meetings, only to burst into tears hours later in her car. She couldn't pinpoint why she felt so overwhelmed until she began to trace the patterns in her behavior. Sarah realized that her habit of suppressing her thoughts and feelings during the day led to a kind of emotional backlog that hit her all at once when she was finally alone.

Reconnecting with your body and emotions requires practice. Start by incorporating small check-ins throughout the day. Ask yourself, "How am I feeling right now?" and "What does my body need?" These moments of self-awareness can help you begin to bridge the gap between your mind and body. Techniques like grounding exercises—such as focusing on your breath or the physical sensation of your feet on the floor—can also help bring you back into the present moment.

Sensory Debt: When Everyday Stimuli Become Threats

For neurodivergent individuals, the world is often an assault on the senses. Fluorescent lights, loud noises, and small talk can feel like physical threats, triggering the nervous system into a state of hyperarousal. When you're masking, this sensory input is compounded by the effort it takes to suppress your natural responses, leading to a phenomenon known as "sensory debt."

Sensory debt occurs when your nervous system becomes overwhelmed by the cumulative impact of everyday stimuli. This hypersensitivity can leave you feeling frazzled, irritable, and exhausted, even after seemingly simple tasks like a trip to the grocery store or a team meeting. It's like running a marathon in flip-flops—your body is constantly bracing itself against discomfort, and it's only a matter of time before you hit a wall.

Understanding your sensory triggers is key to managing this debt. Start by identifying the environments or situations that seem to drain you the most. Is it the hum of fluorescent lights? The chatter of coworkers in an open-plan office? Once you've pinpointed these triggers, you can begin to take steps to mitigate their impact. Noise-canceling headphones, sunglasses, or even a designated quiet space can provide much-needed relief.

Practical Steps to Mitigate Masking

The journey to unmasking begins with small, intentional steps. Reducing sensory overload, reconnecting with your body, and gradually unmasking in safe environments can help you reclaim your neurodivergent brain.

Start by creating a sensory-friendly space where you can retreat when the world feels overwhelming. This might mean dimming the lights, playing soothing music, or surrounding yourself with soft textures. Use this space as a sanctuary where you can let go of the need to mask and simply be yourself.

Next, practice unmasking in low-stakes situations. This could be as simple as allowing yourself to stim during a solo walk or wearing comfortable clothing that doesn't conform to societal expectations. Gradually, you can begin to extend these practices to more challenging environments, building your confidence and resilience along the way.

Finally, prioritize self-compassion. Unmasking is a process, and it's okay to take it one step at a time. Celebrate the small victories, and remind yourself that your worth is not tied to your ability to "look normal."

The physiological toll of masking is real, but so is the potential for healing. By understanding the biological mechanisms behind your symptoms—whether they're rooted in chronic stress, dissociation, or sensory debt—you can begin to take steps toward a more authentic and sustainable way of living. Unmasking isn't about discarding all societal expectations overnight; it's about reclaiming the parts of yourself that have been hidden for too long.

As you move forward, remember that you are not alone in this journey. Countless women are navigating the same challenges, and together, we can create a world where neurodivergent brains are celebrated, not suppressed. Your true self is worth unmasking—step by step, breath by breath.

4

The Cost of Looking Normal

Imagine holding a smile long after your face aches, forcing eye contact when your body screams to look away, or rehearsing a casual conversation until it feels scripted. For neurodivergent individuals, particularly high-achieving women who appear successful on the outside, these are not occasional challenges but daily necessities. The term "masking" describes the practice of concealing autistic or ADHD traits to fit societal norms. While this can help navigate a world designed for neurotypical minds, the toll it takes on the mind and body is immense. This chapter explores the hidden costs of masking, from the strain of forced sociability to the long-term health implications of suppressing natural behaviors. It also offers insights into how to recover from these costs and begin reclaiming your authentic self.

The Strain of Forced Sociability

For many neurodivergent individuals, social interactions are not intuitive but learned performances. Forced eye contact, scripted conversations, and mimicking neurotypical behaviors are strategies that help in appearing "normal." Yet, these practices come at a significant cognitive and emotional cost. Eye contact, for example, can be physically uncomfortable or even painful for many autistic individuals. Research shows that forcing eye contact increases cortisol levels, the body's primary stress hormone, leading to chronic stress over time.

Scripting conversations—rehearsing what to say and how to say it—adds another layer of strain. While this can help navigate social situations, it requires immense mental energy. One woman described scripting as "writing a play in real time while also acting in it." The cognitive load of constantly analyzing social cues and predicting responses can leave little energy for anything else. Over time, this leads to a state of mental exhaustion that many describe as "social burnout."

Personal narratives highlight the real-world impact of these pressures. Sarah, a successful marketing director, shared how she would spend hours preparing for meetings, scripting every possible interaction. While her colleagues saw a confident leader, she felt like an actor perpetually on stage. The cumulative stress led to debilitating migraines and chronic fatigue, forcing her to confront the unsustainable nature of her masking strategies.

The Hidden Toll of Suppressing Stimming

Stimming—short for self-stimulatory behavior—includes actions like hand-flapping, rocking, or finger-tapping. For neurodivergent individuals, stimming is a natural way to regulate sensory input and manage emotional overload. It helps process overwhelming environments and provides a sense of comfort. However, societal pressures often stigmatize these behaviors, leading many to suppress them.

Neuroscientific studies show that stimming plays a crucial role in sensory regulation. When suppressed, the nervous system loses a vital coping mechanism, leading to heightened stress and sensory overload. The consequences of long-term suppression are profound. Without the release provided by stimming, the body accumulates tension, which can manifest as anxiety, irritability, or even physical pain.

Consider the story of Emily, a teacher who prided herself on her ability to "stay calm" in chaotic environments. She suppressed her natural urge to fidget or rock, believing it would make her appear unprofessional. Over time, this led to a constant sense of unease and eventual burnout. When she began allowing herself to stim—even if just tapping her fingers discreetly under her desk—she noticed a significant reduction in her stress levels.

Chronic Illness and Neurological Burnout

The long-term health implications of masking extend beyond stress and fatigue. Sustained suppression of natural behaviors and the constant energy expenditure required to appear neurotypical can lead to chronic illnesses. Conditions such as chronic fatigue syndrome, fibromyalgia, and autoimmune disorders are increasingly linked to prolonged stress and sensory overload. The body's immune system becomes compromised, leaving individuals vulnerable to a range of health issues.

Neurological burnout, a specific condition experienced by many autistic and ADHD individuals, occurs when the brain can no longer process information effectively. Years of masking, suppressing, and overcompensating deplete cognitive reserves, leading to symptoms like memory lapses, sensory sensitivities, and emotional dysregulation. Unfortunately, standard burnout advice—"socialize more," "push through"—often exacerbates the problem by ignoring the neurological roots of the condition.

Medical research supports this connection. Studies have shown that chronic stress disrupts the hypothalamic-pituitary-adrenal (HPA) axis, leading to dysregulation in stress hormone production. This dysregulation contributes to fatigue, pain, and other symptoms associated with chronic illness. For neurodivergent individuals, the additional burden of sensory overload further compounds these effects.

Recovering from the Cost

Recovering from the toll of masking begins with unmasking—gradually allowing yourself to engage in behaviors that feel natural and authentic. This process requires creating environments where neurodivergent needs are respected and accommodated. It might mean wearing noise-canceling headphones in public, allowing yourself to stim, or opting out of social events when necessary.

Practical steps can help ease this transition. Start by identifying situations where masking feels most draining and explore small, manageable changes. For example, if eye contact is uncomfortable, try focusing on the bridge of the nose or explaining your preference to trusted individuals. Gradually reduce the cognitive load of social interactions by letting go of perfectionism—remember, you don't need to script every conversation.

Therapeutic approaches that focus on sensory regulation and self-compassion can also support recovery. Unlike traditional Cognitive Behavioral Therapy (CBT), which often feels invalidating for neurodivergent individuals, therapies like Acceptance and Commitment Therapy (ACT) or sensory integration therapy address the root causes of stress and burnout. These approaches emphasize validating sensory experiences and adapting environments to reduce overload.

Success stories offer hope for recovery. Jessica, a graphic designer, shared how embracing her stimming behaviors—like doodling during meetings—helped her regain focus and reduce anxiety. By altering her workspace to better suit her sensory needs, she found a balance that allowed her creativity to flourish without masking.

The cost of looking normal is steep, particularly for high-achieving neurodivergent women who appear successful but suffer internally. Forced sociability, suppressed stimming, and chronic masking practices wreak havoc on the nervous system, leading to long-term health issues and neurological burnout. However, recovery is possible. By unmasking and adapting environments to better suit neurodivergent needs, individuals can begin reclaiming their authentic selves and improving their health. The journey toward unmasking is not about abandoning societal expectations entirely but about finding a balance that allows you to thrive without sacrificing your well-being. In embracing your neurodivergence, you honor the resilience it has taken to navigate a high-demand world and take the first steps toward a more sustainable, fulfilling life.

5

The Chameleon Effect

For many neurodivergent women, the ability to blend into societal expectations is a survival skill honed over years of practice. This phenomenon, often referred to as masking, involves suppressing natural behaviors and mimicking neurotypical norms to fit in. While masking can offer short-term social acceptance, it comes at a steep cost—dissociation from one's true self, delayed emotional processing, and a profound toll on mental and physical health. This chapter explores the intricate layers of high-masking, particularly among neurodivergent women, and offers pathways toward reclaiming authenticity and neurological well-being.

The Anatomy of Masking

Masking begins early for many neurodivergent women, often as a response to societal pressures and the desire to avoid ostracization. From a young age, they learn to observe and mimic the behaviors of their peers, meticulously crafting a persona that aligns with societal expectations. This chameleon-like adaptability allows them to navigate social situations, excel in academic and professional settings, and maintain relationships. However, the effort required to sustain this facade is immense.

The biological and psychological costs of masking are staggering. Neurologically, masking demands constant vigilance and energy, often leading to sensory overload and cognitive fatigue. Over time, this sustained effort can deplete the brain's resources, resulting in what is now recognized as Autistic/ADHD Burnout—a state where the brain loses its ability to process information efficiently. Psychologically, masking fosters a disconnection from one's true self, creating a void where authenticity should reside. This disconnection often manifests as chronic fatigue, anxiety, and a host of "mystery illnesses" that defy traditional medical explanations.

Dissociation and Delayed Processing

One of the most insidious effects of high-masking is dissociation—a mental state where individuals detach from their emotions, bodily sensations, and even their own identity. For neurodivergent women, this dissociation often manifests as delayed emotional processing. They may not recognize feelings of anger, stress, or sadness until days or even weeks after the triggering event. This delay can lead to prolonged emotional distress and exacerbate anxiety.

The neurological mechanisms behind this delayed processing are complex. When masking, the brain prioritizes survival over emotional integration, pushing aside immediate reactions to focus on maintaining the facade. Over time, this suppression can result in a backlog of unprocessed emotions, which can overwhelm the nervous system. For many women, this manifests as sudden emotional outbursts, unexplained physical symptoms, or a pervasive sense of unease.

Consider the experience of Sarah, a 35-year-old marketing executive diagnosed with ADHD in her early thirties. For years, Sarah prided herself on her ability to "keep it together" in high-pressure environments. However, she often found herself feeling inexplicably drained and irritable after long workdays. It wasn't until she began therapy that she realized her delayed reactions to stress were a result of years of masking. "I would bottle everything up during the day," she shared. "Then, at night, it would hit me like a tidal wave—anger, sadness, exhaustion. I didn't even know where it was coming from."

Case Studies: The Real-Life Impact

The long-term consequences of high-masking are vividly illustrated in the lives of neurodivergent women who have experienced Autistic/ADHD Burnout. Take the case of Emily, a 40-year-old teacher diagnosed with autism in her late thirties. Emily spent decades masking her sensory sensitivities and social differences to succeed in her career. Over time, the cumulative toll of masking led to severe burnout, characterized by chronic fatigue, migraines, and an inability to function at work. It wasn't until she began to unmask—acknowledging her sensory needs and setting boundaries—that she found a path to recovery.

Similarly, Maria, a 29-year-old software developer, experienced years of unexplained physical symptoms before her ADHD diagnosis. "I was always tired, always in pain," she recalled. "Doctors couldn't figure out what was wrong with me." It wasn't until she connected her symptoms to the exhaustion of masking that she began to heal. By prioritizing rest, reducing sensory overload, and embracing her neurodivergent identity, Maria gradually regained her energy and sense of self.

These stories underscore the pervasive impact of masking on physical and mental health. They also highlight the importance of recognizing and addressing the chameleon effect to prevent long-term damage.

Strategies for Mitigating the Chameleon Effect

Recognizing and reducing masking behaviors is a crucial step toward reclaiming authenticity and neurological well-being. One effective strategy is mindfulness practices, which help individuals reconnect with their bodies and emotions. Simple techniques like body scans, deep breathing, and grounding exercises can foster greater awareness of physical sensations and emotional states.

Journaling is another powerful tool for emotional processing. By writing about daily experiences and feelings, individuals can begin to identify patterns and delayed reactions. This practice can create a safe space for processing emotions and reducing the backlog of unexpressed feelings.

Setting boundaries is equally important, particularly in reducing sensory overload. This might involve limiting social interactions, creating quiet spaces at home, or advocating for accommodations at work. For many women, learning to say "no" and prioritize their needs is a transformative step toward unmasking.

Finally, seeking supportive communities and relationships can provide validation and reduce the need for masking. Connecting with other neurodivergent individuals who understand the challenges of high-masking can foster a sense of belonging and authenticity.

Building Authentic Connections

Creating environments that reduce the need for masking is essential for long-term well-being. This includes building supportive relationships and workplaces that accommodate neurodivergent needs. For example, employers can offer flexible work schedules, sensory-friendly spaces, and open communication channels to support neurodivergent employees. In personal relationships, fostering mutual understanding and acceptance can reduce the pressure to mask.

One practical step is to communicate openly about neurodivergent traits and needs. This might involve explaining sensory sensitivities, requesting accommodations, or setting clear expectations in relationships.

By creating spaces where authenticity is valued, individuals can begin to unmask and thrive.

The chameleon effect shapes the lives of many neurodivergent women, often at great personal cost. By understanding the anatomy of masking, recognizing dissociation and delayed processing, and implementing practical strategies, individuals can begin to reclaim their true selves. The journey toward authenticity is not without challenges, but it is a vital step toward neurological well-being and long-term health. Through mindfulness, boundary-setting, and supportive connections, it is possible to unmask and embrace the richness of neurodivergent identity.

6

The Sensory Debt

Imagine walking through a world where every sound is amplified, every light feels like a spotlight, and the texture of your clothing is a constant distraction. For neurodivergent individuals, particularly those who have spent years masking their true selves, this isn't an exaggeration—it's daily life. Sensory overload isn't just discomfort; it's a physiological response that can feel like an unrelenting assault on the nervous system. This chapter explores the concept of Sensory Debt, a state where chronic exposure to unsuitable environments accumulates stress in the body, leading to burnout. By understanding the mechanisms behind sensory processing differences and identifying personal triggers, you can begin to reclaim control over your environment and well-being.

The Physiology of Sensory Overload

To understand why sensory inputs feel like threats, we must first examine how the neurodivergent brain processes stimuli. Unlike neurotypical individuals, whose brains efficiently filter out irrelevant sensory information, neurodivergent brains often struggle with this filtering process. Research suggests that this is due to differences in the thalamus, the brain's sensory gateway, which may allow too much sensory data to pass through unchecked. The result? A nervous system in constant overdrive, interpreting everyday stimuli as potential dangers.

This heightened sensitivity isn't just psychological—it's biological. When sensory input overwhelms the brain, it triggers the fight-or-flight response, flooding the body with stress hormones like cortisol. Over time, this chronic activation leads to Sensory Debt, a cumulative toll on the nervous system. Think of it as a bank account: every time you force yourself to endure fluorescent lights, background chatter, or scratchy fabrics, you withdraw from your limited reserves. Without deposits—moments of sensory relief—the account runs dry, leaving you exhausted, irritable, and unable to function.

Consider the case of Mara, a high-achieving attorney who spent years powering through migraines and fatigue. Only after her autism diagnosis did she realize her symptoms were tied to sensory overload. The hum of office lights, the buzz of conversations, and the stiff blazers she wore to court weren't just annoyances—they were eroding her capacity to think clearly.

Identifying Common Sensory Triggers

Sensory triggers vary widely among individuals, but some patterns emerge. Recognizing your unique sensitivities is the first step toward managing them. Here are some of the most common culprits:

Auditory triggers include overlapping conversations, humming appliances, or sudden loud noises. For many, the din of an open-office workspace can feel like being trapped in a swarm of bees.

Visual triggers often involve bright or flickering lights, cluttered spaces, or rapid movements. Fluorescent lighting, in particular, is a frequent offender, with its harsh glare and imperceptible flicker.

Tactile triggers range from restrictive clothing to unexpected touches. Seams in socks, tags on shirts, or the feeling of certain fabrics can dominate attention, making it impossible to focus on anything else.

Olfactory triggers might include strong perfumes, cleaning products, or cooking smells. For some, these scents are not just unpleasant but physically painful, triggering headaches or nausea.

Take Lena, a teacher who realized her afternoon exhaustion was tied to the school's antiseptic hallway smells. Once she identified this trigger, she began wearing a subtle essential oil blend on her scarf to mask the odor, significantly reducing her fatigue.

The Impact of Sensory Overload on Daily Functioning

When sensory stress goes unmanaged, the consequences ripple through every aspect of life. At work, overload can manifest as difficulty concentrating, missed deadlines, or irritability with colleagues. Socially, it might lead to withdrawing from gatherings or snapping at loved ones. Over time, the toll becomes physical: chronic fatigue, muscle tension, and even autoimmune flare-ups as the body buckles under constant stress.

Many high-masking individuals don't realize their "mystery symptoms" are tied to sensory overwhelm. They blame themselves for being "too sensitive" or push harder, exacerbating the problem. Traditional advice like "just tune it out" or "power through" only deepens the debt. Neurodivergent burnout isn't a matter of willpower—it's a neurological limit.

Strategies for Managing Sensory Debt

The good news? Sensory Debt can be repaid. Start by mapping your triggers. Keep a journal for a week, noting moments of discomfort or fatigue and the sensory inputs present. Patterns will emerge.

Next, create a sensory toolkit. Noise-canceling headphones, tinted glasses, or fidget tools can provide immediate relief. Designate a "sensory safe zone" at home—a quiet, dimly lit space where you can decompress.

Set boundaries unapologetically. If fluorescent lights overwhelm you, request an office with natural light. If fragrances trigger migraines, ask colleagues to avoid heavy perfumes. Your needs are valid.

Finally, schedule sensory breaks. Even five minutes in a quiet space can reset your nervous system. Think of these breaks as deposits into your sensory bank account.

Sensory Debt isn't a life sentence. By honoring your neurological needs instead of suppressing them, you can reduce overwhelm and reclaim your energy. This isn't about self-indulgence—it's about survival. The world may not always accommodate you, but you can build an environment that does. Start small. Identify one trigger today and experiment with one strategy. Over time, these adjustments compound, restoring balance to a system that's been taxed for too long. You deserve a life that doesn't hurt.

7

Step 1: The Low-Dopamine Detox

When you're running on empty—physically, emotionally, and neurologically—it's tempting to grasp for anything that offers a fleeting sense of relief. For many neurodivergent women, this often looks like scrolling endlessly through social media, binge-watching TV, or losing hours to the internet rabbit hole. These behaviors aren't just distractions; they're survival mechanisms. They're your brain's desperate attempt to cope with sensory overwhelm, burnout, and the exhaustion of masking. But while these activities provide a temporary dopamine hit, they come at a cost: they drain your energy, deepen your burnout, and keep you stuck in a cycle of depletion.

This chapter is about breaking that cycle. It's not about shaming yourself for doom scrolling or labeling your habits as "bad." Instead, it's about understanding why your brain craves these quick fixes and how you can replace them with strategies that nourish your nervous system instead of depleting it. Welcome to the Low-Dopamine Detox—the first step in reclaiming your neurodivergent brain and finding sustainable ways to thrive in a high-demand world.

Why Dopamine Detox Matters

Dopamine is often misunderstood. It's not just the "feel-good" chemical; it's a neurotransmitter that plays a critical role in motivation, focus, and reward processing. For neurodivergent brains, dopamine regulation works differently. Many people with ADHD, for example, have lower baseline levels of dopamine, which can make it harder to feel motivated or sustained by everyday tasks. Autism, too, often involves unique sensory processing needs that can leave the brain craving stimulation—or relief—in ways that feel out of sync with the neurotypical world.

When you're masking—suppressing your natural behaviors to fit societal expectations—your brain is working overtime. This constant effort depletes your dopamine reserves even further, leaving you vulnerable to burnout. To cope, you might turn to activities like doom scrolling or binge-watching. These behaviors offer quick dopamine hits, but they're like junk food for your brain: satisfying in the moment but ultimately unfulfilling. Worse, they can lead to a phenomenon known as "sensory debt," where the sensory input you're avoiding (because it's overwhelming) builds up, leaving you even more depleted.

A Low-Dopamine Detox isn't about cutting out every source of pleasure or stimulation. It's about identifying the activities that drain you and replacing them with ones that restore balance. It's about understanding your brain's unique needs and giving it the kind of nourishment—sensory, emotional, and neurological—that allows you to thrive.

Doom Scrolling as a Stim

For many neurodivergent women, doom scrolling isn't just a habit—it's a stim. Stimming, or self-stimulatory behavior, is a natural way for neurodivergent brains to regulate sensory input and process emotions. While stimming is often associated with physical actions like hand-flapping or rocking, it can also take less obvious forms, like scrolling through social media or obsessively reading news articles.

Doom scrolling provides a kind of sensory feedback loop. The endless stream of information can be soothing in a chaotic world—a way to feel connected, occupied, or distracted from overwhelming emotions. But like many stims, it's a double-edged sword. While it offers temporary relief, it also keeps your brain in a heightened state of arousal, making it harder to rest and recover.

Consider Sarah, a 35-year-old marketing executive with ADHD and autism. Sarah found herself scrolling through Instagram late into the night, even though she knew it was making her more tired. "It felt like I couldn't stop," she shared. "I was exhausted, but I kept telling myself one more post, one more video. It was like I was trying to calm myself down, but it just made everything worse."

Sarah's experience is common. Doom scrolling isn't a moral failing or a lack of willpower; it's a coping mechanism. The key is to recognize it as such and find healthier ways to meet the same needs.

The Cost of Cheap Dopamine

The problem with cheap dopamine sources—like social media, video games, or binge-watching—isn't just that they're unproductive. It's that they hijack your brain's reward system, creating a cycle of craving and depletion. Every time you engage in these activities, your brain releases a flood of dopamine, reinforcing the behavior. But because these hits are short-lived, you're left craving more, even as your energy and focus plummet.

Over time, this cycle can have serious consequences. It can exacerbate sensory overwhelm, making it harder to tolerate everyday stimuli. It can impair executive function, leaving you feeling scattered and overwhelmed. And it can heighten anxiety, as your brain becomes increasingly reliant on external sources of stimulation.

Breaking this cycle isn't easy, but it's essential. Research shows that reducing reliance on cheap dopamine sources can help restore your brain's natural balance, improving focus, energy, and emotional regulation. The key is to replace these habits with activities that provide sustainable dopamine release—activities that nourish rather than deplete.

Sensory Regulation Techniques

Replacing cheap dopamine with healthier alternatives starts with understanding your sensory needs. For neurodivergent brains, sensory regulation is often the missing piece of the puzzle. When your sensory system is balanced, your brain functions better, and you're less likely to seek out quick fixes.

Grounding exercises are a powerful tool for sensory regulation. Practices like deep breathing, progressive muscle relaxation, or mindfulness can help calm an overstimulated nervous system. Sensory-friendly activities—like weighted blankets, fidget toys, or listening to calming music—can also provide soothing input without overloading your brain.

It's important to personalize these strategies to fit your unique sensory profile. If you're sensory-seeking, activities like rocking, bouncing on a yoga ball, or chewing gum might help. If you're sensory-avoidant, you might prefer quiet, low-stimulation activities like knitting or spending time in nature. The key is to experiment and find what works for you.

Building a Low-Dopamine Routine

Creating a sustainable Low-Dopamine Routine starts with setting boundaries with technology. This might mean designating specific times for social media, turning off notifications, or using apps that limit screen time. It's not about cutting out technology entirely but about using it intentionally.

Incorporating sensory breaks into your day is also crucial. These breaks don't have to be long—even a few minutes of deep breathing or stretching can make a difference. The goal is to give your brain regular opportunities to reset and recharge.

Finally, it's important to integrate these practices into your daily life in a way that feels manageable. Start small, focusing on one or two changes at a time. Celebrate your progress, and be gentle with yourself when setbacks occur. Remember, this isn't about perfection; it's about progress.

The Low-Dopamine Detox is more than just a wellness trend; it's a lifeline for neurodivergent brains navigating a high-demand world. By reducing your reliance on cheap dopamine sources and replacing them with sensory-regulation techniques, you can begin to restore balance and reclaim your energy. This process isn't about shame or self-denial; it's about understanding your brain's unique needs and giving it the care it deserves. Take it one step at a time, and remember: you're not alone in this journey. With patience and compassion, you can create a life that feels nourishing, sustainable, and authentically yours.

8

Step 2: Mapping Your Sensory Profile

If you've ever felt overwhelmed by the hum of fluorescent lights, the scratch of a wool sweater, or the disorienting sensation of riding an escalator, you're not alone. For neurodivergent individuals, sensory sensitivities are more than just minor annoyances—they can significantly impact daily functioning, contributing to exhaustion, burnout, and a sense of being perpetually out of sync with the world. This chapter is designed to help you understand and map your unique sensory profile, providing you with the tools to reclaim control over your sensory environment and, ultimately, your neurodivergent brain.

Understanding Sensory Sensitivity

Sensory sensitivity is a cornerstone of neurodivergence, particularly for those with ADHD and Autism. Unlike neurotypical individuals, whose nervous systems filter sensory input efficiently, neurodivergent brains often process sensory information more intensely. This heightened sensitivity can manifest in various ways—some individuals may be hypersensitive to certain stimuli, while others may seek out sensory input to regulate their nervous systems. Common triggers include bright lights, loud noises, strong smells, and tactile sensations like clothing tags or rough textures.

To understand why this happens, let's briefly explore the science. The nervous system acts as a gatekeeper for sensory information, determining which stimuli to prioritize and which to filter out. In neurodivergent individuals, this gatekeeping system operates differently, often leading to sensory overload or understimulation. For example, the vestibular system, which controls balance and spatial orientation, can be particularly sensitive in Autistic individuals, making activities like riding in a car or navigating crowded spaces feel overwhelming. Similarly, auditory sensitivities can make everyday sounds like chewing or a ringing phone feel unbearable.

Understanding your sensory sensitivities is the first step toward managing them. When you're aware of how your nervous system responds to different stimuli, you can make intentional choices to reduce sensory overwhelm and create a more supportive environment.

Identifying Your Sensory Profile

Mapping your sensory profile begins with self-awareness. This process involves identifying which sensory inputs trigger discomfort or stress and which bring comfort or calm. To help you get started, consider the following self-assessment tools and guided reflections.

First, focus on the three primary sensory categories: vestibular, auditory, and tactile. Vestibular sensitivity relates to balance and movement—do you feel dizzy or disoriented when you ride in a car or spin around? Auditory sensitivity involves how you process sound—do you find yourself covering your ears in noisy environments or becoming irritated by repetitive noises? Tactile sensitivity pertains to touch—do certain fabrics, textures, or physical sensations feel intolerable?

Next, take a moment to reflect on your daily experiences. Notice when you feel overwhelmed or fatigued—what sensory inputs were present at those times? Conversely, think about moments when you feel calm and centered—what sensory elements contributed to that state? Keeping a sensory journal can be an invaluable tool for tracking these patterns over time.

Workshop Exercises: Practical Application

To help you dive deeper into mapping your sensory profile, let's explore a series of practical workshop exercises. These activities are designed to help you identify and understand your sensory triggers and preferences.

1. Sensory Journaling: For one week, jot down your sensory experiences each day. Note any moments of discomfort or overwhelm, as well as instances of comfort or calm. Pay attention to the sensory input involved—was it a loud noise, a particular texture, or a specific movement? Over time, patterns will emerge, helping you identify your key sensitivities.

2. Environmental Audit: Take a close look at the spaces where you spend the most time—your home, workplace, or car. Consider the sensory elements present: lighting, noise levels, smells, and textures. Are there any patterns that correlate with your moments of overwhelm? For example, do fluorescent lights or strong scents consistently trigger discomfort? Make notes of these observations.

3. Sensory Experiments: Try exposing yourself to different sensory stimuli in a controlled way to test your reactions. For example, listen to various frequencies of sound, touch different textures, or try gentle movements like rocking or swaying. Pay attention to how your body and mind respond—what feels soothing, and what feels overwhelming?

These exercises are not about forcing yourself to endure uncomfortable stimuli but rather about gathering information to inform your choices moving forward.

Managing Sensory Sensitivities

Once you've identified your sensory triggers, the next step is to develop strategies for managing them. Here are some practical tips to help you create a sensory-friendly environment and communicate your needs effectively.

1. Create Sensory-Friendly Spaces: Start by modifying your immediate surroundings to reduce sensory overload. Use soft lighting instead of harsh fluorescents, invest in noise-canceling headphones, and choose clothing with comfortable textures. If possible, designate a quiet, calming space where you can retreat when feeling overwhelmed.

2. Use Sensory Regulation Tools: Experiment with tools that help regulate your nervous system. Weighted blankets, fidget toys, or calming essential oils can provide soothing sensory input. Similarly, activities like deep breathing, yoga, or gentle rocking can help restore balance when you're feeling dysregulated.

3. Communicate Your Needs: Advocating for your sensory needs is essential, especially in shared spaces like work or family environments. Be clear and specific about what accommodations would help—whether it's requesting a quieter workspace, asking for noise-reducing headphones, or explaining why certain textures or smells are triggering. Remember, your needs are valid, and communicating them is an act of self-care.

Case Studies and Real-Life Examples

To illustrate the power of mapping and managing sensory profiles, let's explore a few real-life examples. Meet Emily, a successful marketing executive who struggled with chronic fatigue and migraines for years. Through sensory journaling, she discovered that fluorescent lighting and noisy open-office environments were major triggers. By transitioning to a remote work setup and using noise-canceling headphones, she was able to reduce her sensory overwhelm dramatically.

Then there's Sarah, a mother of two who felt constantly on edge at home. An environmental audit revealed that the chaotic noise levels and overwhelming clutter in her living space were contributing to her stress. By decluttering her home and creating a designated quiet corner, Sarah found a renewed sense of calm.

These stories highlight the transformative impact of understanding and addressing sensory sensitivities. While everyone's journey is unique, the common thread is empowerment—by taking control of their sensory environments, these individuals were able to reclaim their energy and well-being.

Mapping your sensory profile is not just an exercise in self-awareness—it's a powerful tool for reclaiming your neurodivergent brain in a high-demand world. By understanding how your nervous system processes sensory input, you can make intentional choices to reduce overwhelm and create a more supportive environment. Whether it's through sensory journaling, environmental audits, or sensory experiments, the process of identifying and managing your sensitivities is deeply personal and profoundly transformative.

Remember, your sensory needs are valid, and honoring them is an essential part of self-care. As you move through this chapter and begin to map your sensory profile, approach the process with curiosity and compassion. You're not just identifying triggers—you're building a foundation for a life that feels more aligned, balanced, and authentically yours. Let this be the step that empowers you to thrive, unmasked and unapologetically neurodivergent.

9

Step 3: The No Audit

In a world that often demands more than we can give, especially for neurodivergent individuals, the ability to discern between what we can do and what we should do becomes critical. This chapter introduces the concept of the 'No Audit,' a transformative tool designed to help you reclaim your energy, reduce sensory overload, and honor your neurological needs. For those who have spent years masking—suppressing natural behaviors to fit societal norms—this process is not just about saying no; it's about saying yes to yourself. By differentiating between preferences and physical needs, understanding the science behind sensory overload, and learning to communicate boundaries effectively, you can move from chronic burnout to sustainable well-being.

Understanding the Difference Between Preferences and Needs

One of the most insidious challenges for neurodivergent individuals is the tendency to mislabel physical and emotional needs as mere preferences. Society often teaches us to push through discomfort, framing our needs as inconveniences or weaknesses. For example, you might tell yourself that skipping a loud social event is a "preference" rather than acknowledging that the noise will leave you physically drained. This misclassification leads to chronic burnout, as you repeatedly ignore your body's signals in favor of external expectations.

To begin addressing this, it's essential to practice self-awareness. Start by reflecting on daily activities and rating them based on how they make you feel physically and emotionally. For instance, attending a crowded meeting may leave you with a headache or heightened anxiety, while a quiet walk might feel rejuvenating. These distinctions are not about disliking certain tasks; they're about recognizing how your nervous system responds to stimuli.

Practical exercises can help clarify these differences. Try keeping a sensory journal for a week, noting your energy levels before and after specific activities. Pay attention to signs of fatigue, irritability, or physical discomfort. Over time, patterns will emerge, helping you identify which activities are truly harmful versus those that are simply undesirable.

The Science Behind Sensory Overload

Sensory overload is not a sign of weakness; it's a neurological reality for many neurodivergent individuals. Research shows that ADHD and Autism often involve heightened sensory processing, meaning the brain struggles to filter out irrelevant stimuli. When compounded by years of masking—forcing yourself to engage in behaviors that feel unnatural—this can lead to sensory debt. Sensory debt occurs when the nervous system becomes hypersensitive, making even minor stimuli feel overwhelming.

For example, one study found that Autistic individuals experience prolonged activation of the sympathetic nervous system (the "fight or flight" response) in response to everyday stressors. This contrasts with neurotypical individuals, who can often recover more quickly. Case studies illustrate how sensory debt manifests in daily life: a high-masking woman might push through a busy workday, only to collapse into exhaustion afterward, unable to function for hours or even days. Traditional advice like "push through" or "socialize more" exacerbates this issue, as it fails to account for neurological differences.

Understanding this science is empowering. It validates your experiences and highlights the importance of addressing sensory needs proactively. By recognizing the toll that certain activities take on your nervous system, you can make informed decisions about where to invest your energy.

Conducting Your 'No Audit'

The 'No Audit' is a structured process designed to help you evaluate commitments and identify which ones are harmful. It involves assessing activities based on their physical and emotional impact, rather than societal expectations or guilt. Here's how to get started:

1. Create a List: Write down all your regular commitments, from work tasks to social obligations.
2. Rate Each Item: Use a scale of 1 to 10 to rate how each activity affects your energy levels.
3. Identify Patterns: Look for activities that consistently drain you or trigger sensory overload.
4. Prioritize: Decide which commitments are essential and which can be reduced or eliminated.

Tools like sensory journals and activity logs can enhance this process. For example, one woman discovered that attending weekly family dinners left her feeling irritable and exhausted. By tracking her responses, she realized it was the combination of noise and social demands that overwhelmed her. With this insight, she proposed a quieter, less frequent gathering, which improved her well-being and strengthened her relationships.

Communicating Boundaries Without Guilt

Setting boundaries is essential for reducing burnout, but it can feel daunting, especially if you fear conflict or judgment. Many high-masking individuals worry that saying no will make them appear lazy or selfish. However, communicating boundaries is not about rejecting others; it's about preserving your ability to show up authentically in your relationships.

Effective communication starts with clarity. Instead of offering vague excuses, be direct and specific. For example, rather than saying, "I'm too busy," you might say, "I need to limit my social commitments to protect my energy." Frame your boundaries as acts of self-care, not rejection.

Scripts can be especially helpful for navigating challenging conversations. For instance:

- "I value our time together, but I need to leave early to recharge."
- "I can't take on this project right now, but I'd be happy to help with something smaller."

Case studies demonstrate how setting boundaries can improve relationships. One woman, fearful of disappointing her coworkers, initially hesitated to decline additional tasks. However, when she explained her need for balance, her team responded with understanding and support.

Case Studies: Real-Life Applications of the 'No Audit'

Real-life examples bring the 'No Audit' to life, showcasing its transformative potential. Each case study highlights specific challenges and the tangible benefits of implementing this process.

For instance, Sarah, a high-masking professional, struggled with chronic fatigue and migraines. Through her 'No Audit,' she discovered that attending networking events was a significant trigger. By replacing these events with smaller, quieter gatherings, she reduced her sensory debt and regained her energy.

Another case involves Maria, a mother of two, who felt overwhelmed by her family's demands. Her 'No Audit' revealed that driving her children to multiple activities was depleting her reserves. By enlisting her partner's help and limiting extracurricular commitments, she created more time for rest and self-care.

These stories illustrate that the 'No Audit' is not about eliminating all obligations; it's about aligning your commitments with your neurological needs.

The 'No Audit' is a powerful tool for reclaiming your neurodivergent brain in a high-demand world. By differentiating between preferences and needs, understanding the science behind sensory overload, and communicating boundaries effectively, you can reduce burnout and honor your unique way of being. This process is not about perfection; it's about progress. Each small step toward prioritizing your well-being brings you closer to a sustainable, fulfilling life.

As you embark on this journey, remember that saying no to what drains you is saying yes to yourself. It's an act of self-respect, not selfishness. By embracing the 'No Audit,' you reclaim your energy, your time, and your right to live authentically.

10

The 80/20 Rule of Unmasking

For many neurodivergent women, the journey toward authenticity feels like a tightrope walk. On one side lies the need to survive in a world designed for neurotypical brains—holding down jobs, managing families, and meeting societal expectations. On the other side is the deep longing to finally shed the masks that have protected but also suffocated them for years. The truth is, unmasking doesn't have to be an all-or-nothing endeavor. It's not about tossing aside every coping mechanism overnight but rather about finding a balance that honors your needs without sacrificing your ability to function in a high-demand world. This is where the 80/20 Rule of Unmasking comes in.

Understanding the 80/20 Rule

The 80/20 Rule, also known as the Pareto Principle, suggests that 80% of outcomes often come from 20% of efforts. When applied to unmasking, this means focusing the majority of your energy on environments where it's safe to be your authentic self, while reserving a smaller portion for settings where masking may still feel necessary. For example, you might unmask fully at home with trusted loved ones but choose to maintain a more reserved demeanor at work or in public.

This approach is particularly important for women experiencing autistic/ADHD burnout, where the brain's capacity to process information has been depleted by years of suppressing natural behaviors. Unmasking everywhere, all at once, is not only unrealistic but could also lead to further overwhelm. Instead, selective vulnerability allows you to conserve energy and prioritize spaces where unmasking will have the most significant impact on your well-being.

Consider Maya, a high-achieving attorney who was recently diagnosed with autism in her late 30s. After years of masking her sensory sensitivities and social differences, she was on the brink of burnout. By applying the 80/20 Rule, Maya began unmasking at home first—telling her partner about her need for quiet evenings to recharge, allowing herself to stim freely, and creating a sensory-friendly environment. At work, she continued to mask in meetings but started setting boundaries around her workload and advocating for accommodations like noise-canceling headphones. Over time, Maya found that this balance reduced her exhaustion and allowed her to feel more like herself.

Mapping Your Masking Tendencies

Before you can unmask strategically, you need to understand where and how you're masking most frequently. This begins with a self-assessment exercise designed to help you identify the behaviors, situations, and environments that drain your energy the most. Start by categorizing your masking tendencies into broad areas: social (e.g., forcing eye contact, suppressing stims), sensory (e.g., enduring bright lights or loud noises), and emotional (e.g., hiding overwhelm or anxiety).

Next, create a "masking map" by listing the places or situations where these behaviors occur most often. For instance, you might notice that masking spikes during work meetings, family gatherings, or crowded public spaces. Once you've mapped out these tendencies, prioritize the areas where unmasking would have the greatest positive impact on your energy and mental health.

For example, Sarah, a marketing executive with ADHD, realized she was masking heavily during client presentations by suppressing her natural enthusiasm for fear of being seen as "too much." By identifying this tendency, she decided to unmask selectively by allowing herself to show more excitement during internal team meetings, where she felt safer. This small shift helped her preserve energy for high-pressure client interactions while gradually embracing authenticity in other areas.

Creating Safe Spaces for Unmasking

One of the most powerful steps in the unmasking process is designing environments where you feel safe to be your true self. This begins with clear communication about your needs to the people closest to you. For instance, you might explain to your family that you need a quiet space to decompress after work or ask a trusted friend to accommodate your sensory sensitivities when planning outings.

Modifying physical spaces can also make unmasking more sustainable. This might involve creating a sensory-friendly corner in your home with soft lighting, comfortable seating, and noise-reducing elements or advocating for workplace adjustments like a quieter desk location or flexible work hours.

Consider Emma, a mother of two who was experiencing burnout from years of masking her autistic traits. She began by transforming her bedroom into a sensory sanctuary, replacing harsh overhead lights with soft lamps and introducing weighted blankets and noise machines. She also communicated her needs to her partner, explaining that she required uninterrupted downtime each evening to recharge. These changes allowed Emma to unmask more freely at home, providing a crucial foundation for her journey toward authenticity.

Gradual Unmasking in Professional Settings

Unmasking at work can feel particularly daunting, as professional environments often demand conformity and suppress individuality. However, small, strategic steps can help you balance authenticity with professionalism without jeopardizing your career.

Start by setting boundaries that protect your energy. This might involve declining optional meetings, blocking off time for focused work, or using tools like email autoresponders to manage communication. Advocating for accommodations, such as flexible deadlines or a quieter workspace, can also reduce the need to mask constantly.

Another effective strategy is selectively unmasking in low-stakes situations. For example, you might allow yourself to stim discreetly during team brainstorming sessions or share a personal interest with a close colleague. These small acts of authenticity can create a ripple effect, increasing your comfort with unmasking over time.

Take Anna, a project manager with ADHD, who struggled with masking her impulsivity and hyperactivity at work. She began by allowing herself to fidget discreetly during meetings and gradually started sharing more about her creative ideas with her team. Over time, these small changes helped Anna feel more aligned with her true self while maintaining her professional reputation.

Building a Sustainable Unmasking Practice

Unmasking is not a one-time event but an ongoing practice that requires self-compassion, energy conservation, and gradual progress. Start by setting realistic goals based on your masking map and prioritize areas where unmasking will have the most significant impact. Celebrate small victories along the way, whether it's allowing yourself to stim in public or advocating for an accommodation at work.

Monitor your progress regularly, adjusting your strategies as needed. If certain unmasking efforts feel too overwhelming, scale back and focus on smaller steps. Remember, the goal is not perfection but progress. Build a support system of trusted friends, family members, or neurodivergent communities who can encourage and validate your journey.

Above all, practice self-compassion. Unmasking after years of suppression is a courageous act, and it's okay to stumble along the way. Treat yourself with the same kindness and understanding you would offer a close friend navigating a similar path.

The 80/20 Rule of Unmasking offers a practical framework for balancing authenticity with the demands of a high-pressure world. By focusing your unmasking efforts on safe, supportive environments and strategically navigating more challenging settings, you can reduce burnout and reclaim your true self without sacrificing your ability to function. Remember, unmasking is not about shedding every mask at once but about finding a sustainable balance that honors your needs and allows you to thrive. As you embark on this journey, take it one step at a time, celebrate your progress, and trust that the path toward authenticity is worth every effort.

11

Designing a Low-Demand Lifestyle

Living with a neurodivergent brain in a world designed for neurotypical individuals often feels like running a marathon without proper training. The constant demands on executive function, sensory overload, and societal expectations can leave you feeling drained and disconnected from your true self. This chapter is about reclaiming your energy and designing a lifestyle that aligns with your neurological needs. By reducing daily demands, creating sensory-friendly spaces, and simplifying routines, you can begin to heal from Autistic/ADHD burnout and rediscover a sense of balance and calm.

The Power of Automation

Automation is a lifeline for neurodivergent brains. It reduces the cognitive load of mundane tasks, allowing you to conserve mental energy for what truly matters. Start by identifying tasks that feel overwhelming or repetitive. These could include meal preparation, bill payments, or household chores. Once you've pinpointed these tasks, explore tools and services that can streamline them.

Smart home devices like programmable thermostats, robotic vacuum cleaners, and voice-activated assistants can simplify daily life. Apps for meal planning and grocery delivery can take the stress out of cooking, while automatic bill payments ensure you never miss a due date. Setting up reminders for medication or appointments can also help reduce anxiety about forgetting important tasks.

The goal of automation isn't just efficiency; it's about creating space for rest and creativity. By offloading these responsibilities, you free up mental bandwidth to focus on activities that bring joy and fulfillment.

Sensory-Friendly Spaces

Your environment plays a significant role in your well-being. Sensory-friendly spaces can help minimize overload and create a sense of safety. Begin by assessing your surroundings: Is there visual clutter that distracts you? Are lights too harsh or noise levels too high? Small adjustments can make a big difference.

Consider reducing visual clutter by organizing items into bins or drawers with clear labels. Soft, diffused lighting can replace harsh overhead lights, and noise-canceling headphones or white noise machines can help manage auditory distractions. If possible, designate a "safe space" in your home—a quiet, comfortable area where you can retreat when feeling overwhelmed.

At work, advocate for accommodations like a quieter workspace or the option to wear noise-canceling headphones. If you're unable to make physical changes, even small adjustments—like positioning your desk away from high-traffic areas—can help create a more sensory-friendly environment.

Simplifying Daily Routines

Complex routines can quickly become overwhelming. Simplifying your daily tasks can reduce stress and make life more manageable. Start by breaking down routines into smaller, actionable steps. For example, instead of "clean the kitchen," create a checklist with specific tasks like "wash dishes," "wipe counters," and "empty the trash."

Visual aids like calendars, planners, and checklists can help you stay organized and reduce decision fatigue. Prioritize tasks based on importance and energy levels, and don't be afraid to delegate or postpone less urgent responsibilities. Setting realistic goals is key—overcommitting can lead to burnout, while manageable tasks promote a sense of accomplishment.

Remember, simplicity is subjective. What works for one person may not work for another. Experiment with different approaches until you find a routine that feels sustainable and supportive.

Communicating Your Needs

Advocating for yourself can feel daunting, especially if you've spent years masking your true self. However, communicating your needs is essential for creating a low-demand lifestyle. Start by identifying specific challenges—whether they're sensory sensitivities, executive function difficulties, or the need for downtime.

When explaining these needs to others, focus on clarity and assertiveness. Use simple, straightforward language to describe how certain accommodations can improve your well-being. For example, "I need a quiet space to decompress after work" or "I find it easier to focus when I have sensory breaks."

Setting boundaries is equally important. It's okay to say no to social events or responsibilities that drain your energy. Remember, your needs are valid, and advocating for them isn't selfish—it's an act of self-care.

Reclaiming Energy Through Rest

Rest is not a luxury; it's a necessity. For neurodivergent individuals, intentional rest is crucial for recovering from the demands of daily life. Begin by scheduling downtime into your routine. This could include short sensory breaks throughout the day or longer periods of rest on weekends.

Mindfulness practices, such as deep breathing or meditation, can help calm an overactive nervous system. Activities like reading, knitting, or listening to music can also serve as restorative hobbies. The key is to prioritize activities that feel genuinely restful to you, rather than following societal expectations of "relaxation."

It's also important to reframe rest as an active, intentional choice rather than a sign of laziness. Rest is where healing happens, and allowing yourself this time is a powerful step toward recovery.

Designing a low-demand lifestyle is about more than productivity hacks or organizational tips—it's about creating a life that respects and supports your neurodivergent brain. By automating routine tasks, crafting sensory-friendly spaces, simplifying daily routines, communicating your needs, and prioritizing rest, you can begin to reclaim your energy and authenticity.

Remember, this journey is deeply personal. What works for someone else may not work for you, and that's okay. The goal is to experiment, adapt, and find strategies that feel sustainable and empowering. Above all, be kind to yourself. Healing from burnout is a gradual process, but every small change brings you closer to a life that feels aligned with your true self. This chapter is your invitation to take that first step—to design a lifestyle that honors who you are and allows you to thrive.

12

Re-parenting the Neurospicy Child Within

Re-parenting the Neurospicy Child Within

For many neurodivergent women, the journey to self-acceptance often begins with a reckoning: the realization that the person they've spent years trying to be is not who they truly are. Beneath the layers of masking, accommodation, and high achievement lies a child—a neurospicy child—whose needs were misunderstood, ignored, or even punished. Re-parenting this inner child is not just an act of self-care; it's a profound act of reclamation. In this chapter, we'll explore how to nurture and heal the neurospicy child within, addressing internalized shame, reframing misconceptions, and cultivating self-compassion to break free from the cycle of burnout.

Understanding the Neurospicy Child

The neurospicy child is a metaphor for the neurodivergent traits and needs that were suppressed during childhood. For many high-masking women, these traits—such as intense focus, sensory sensitivities, or a need for deep connection—were labeled as problematic. Think of the young girl who was told to sit still when she needed to move, or the teen who was scolded for being "too sensitive" when she felt overwhelmed by noise. These experiences create a disconnect between who we are and who we're told we should be.

Take Sarah, for example. As a child, she loved organizing her toys into intricate systems, but her parents dismissed this as "wasting time." In adulthood, Sarah became a successful project manager, but she struggled with chronic exhaustion and feelings of inadequacy. It wasn't until her ADHD diagnosis that she realized her childhood love of organizing wasn't frivolous—it was a natural expression of her neurodivergence. By reconnecting with her neurospicy child, Sarah began to see her traits not as flaws but as strengths.

The suppression of the neurospicy child often leads to internalized shame. This shame doesn't disappear in adulthood; it morphs into feelings of being "too much" or "not enough." It's the voice that whispers, "Why can't you just keep up?" or "You're just lazy." To heal, we must first understand where these narratives come from and how they've shaped our lives.

Shame and Its Roots

Shame is a heavy burden for many neurodivergent women, especially those who have spent years masking their true selves. This shame often stems from childhood experiences where neurodivergent traits were misunderstood or punished. For example, a child who needed extra time to process information might have been labeled "slow" or "difficult." A teen who struggled with social cues might have been told she was "rude" or "awkward." These labels become internalized, shaping our self-perception.

High-masking women often carry this shame into adulthood, where it manifests as chronic feelings of inadequacy. We push ourselves to excel in careers, relationships, and parenting, yet we still feel like we're falling short. This isn't because we're failing; it's because we're trying to meet neurotypical standards with neurodivergent brains.

To dismantle these shame narratives, we must first identify them. Start by reflecting on the messages you received as a child. What words were used to describe your behavior? How did those words make you feel? Once you've identified these narratives, challenge them. Ask yourself, "Is this really true? Or is this just a story I've been told?" For example, if you were told you were "lazy," consider whether what was labeled as laziness might actually have been your brain's way of conserving energy.

Reframing Laziness: Energy Conservation

The societal notion of laziness is particularly damaging for neurodivergent individuals. What's often labeled as laziness is actually a necessary form of energy conservation. Neurodivergent brains process information differently, which can be mentally exhausting. Masking—trying to appear "normal"—amplifies this exhaustion, leading to chronic fatigue and burnout.

Consider Emma, who spent years working overtime to prove she wasn't "lazy." Despite her success, she was constantly exhausted and struggled with migraines. After her autism diagnosis, Emma realized that what she'd labeled as laziness was her brain's way of saying, "I need rest." By reframing laziness as energy conservation, she began to prioritize rest without guilt.

Managing energy effectively starts with understanding your limits. Pay attention to your body's signals. Do you feel overstimulated after socializing? Do certain tasks drain your energy more than others? Once you've identified these patterns, create an energy budget. Allocate your energy to high-priority tasks and allow yourself to rest when needed. Remember, rest isn't a luxury; it's a necessity.

Practical Exercises for Self-Compassion

Self-compassion is a powerful tool for healing the neurospicy child within. It involves treating yourself with the same kindness and understanding you'd offer a friend. For neurodivergent women, this can be challenging, especially if you've spent years criticizing yourself. But with practice, self-compassion becomes a habit.

One effective exercise is guided meditation. Find a quiet space and visualize your neurospicy child. What does she look like? What does she need? Offer her words of comfort and reassurance. Journaling is another helpful practice. Write a letter to your younger self, acknowledging her struggles and celebrating her strengths.

Sensory-based self-care activities can also foster self-compassion. For example, if you're feeling overwhelmed, try wrapping yourself in a weighted blanket or listening to calming music. These activities ground you in the present moment and remind you that your needs matter.

Building a Compassionate Relationship with Yourself

Re-parenting the neurospicy child within is ultimately about building a compassionate relationship with yourself. This involves recognizing and celebrating your neurodivergent traits, setting boundaries, and creating a supportive environment.

Start by identifying what brings you joy. Maybe it's immersing yourself in a special interest or spending time in nature. Make space for these activities in your life. Next, set boundaries to protect your energy. This might mean saying no to social events or delegating tasks at work. Remember, setting boundaries isn't selfish; it's self-respect.

Finally, surround yourself with people who understand and support you. This might include joining a neurodivergent support group or connecting with like-minded friends. Building a compassionate relationship with yourself is an ongoing process, but with time and practice, it becomes second nature.

Conclusion

Re-parenting the neurospicy child within is a journey of self-discovery and healing. By addressing internalized shame, reframing misconceptions, and cultivating self-compassion, you can break free from the cycle of burnout and embrace your authentic self. Remember, your neurodivergence isn't a flaw; it's a fundamental part of who you are. As you nurture your neurospicy child, you'll find the courage to unmask, reclaim your energy, and live a life that truly reflects your unique brilliance.

13

Moving from Surviving to Glimmers

For many neurodivergent individuals, especially those who have spent years masking their true selves, life can feel like a relentless cycle of survival. The weight of high-demand environments—be it work, family, or social obligations—can leave you feeling drained, disconnected, and stuck in a state of perpetual burnout. But what if there were tiny, accessible moments of joy that could help you shift from merely surviving to truly thriving? These moments, known as glimmers, are micro-experiences of joy, calm, or sensory pleasure that can act as lifelines in your daily life.

Glimmers are not grand, life-altering events. They are small, often overlooked pleasures—the warmth of sunlight on your skin, the hum of a favorite song, the scent of fresh coffee. For neurodivergent individuals experiencing burnout, these moments are especially vital. They can help recalibrate your nervous system, reduce stress, and provide a sense of grounding. This chapter will guide you through understanding glimmers, identifying your own, and integrating them into your daily life to foster long-term well-being.

Understanding Glimmers: The Neuroscience Behind Micro-Moments of Joy

Glimmers are deeply rooted in neuroscience. Unlike the fight-or-flight response triggered by stress, glimmers activate the parasympathetic nervous system, which promotes relaxation and restoration. When you experience a glimmer, your brain releases neurotransmitters like dopamine and endorphins, which counteract the effects of cortisol, the stress hormone.

Recent studies have shown that glimmers are particularly beneficial for neurodivergent individuals. For example, research indicates that sensory-based positive experiences can help regulate sensory processing, which is often dysregulated in neurodivergent brains. These moments can also reduce the impact of chronic stress, which is a key contributor to burnout.

Consider the case of Maya, a high-achieving professional with ADHD. She often felt overwhelmed by the demands of her job and the sensory overload of her environment. After learning about glimmers, Maya began to notice how the tactile sensation of her favorite sweater or the sound of birdsong outside her window could instantly calm her. These tiny moments didn't solve her problems, but they gave her brief respites that made her days more manageable.

Identifying Your Glimmers: A Self-Discovery Exercise

The first step in cultivating glimmers is identifying what brings you joy or calm. This requires a mindful, sensory-focused approach. Begin by creating a sensory map: a simple exercise where you explore your five senses to pinpoint what feels soothing or pleasurable.

For example, think about touch. Does the texture of a soft blanket bring you comfort? How about the sensation of warm water on your hands? For sound, consider whether certain music, nature sounds, or even silence feels calming. For smell, identify scents that make you feel grounded, such as lavender, citrus, or baking bread.

Keep a journal dedicated to recording these discoveries. Write down moments when you feel even a flicker of joy or calm. Over time, patterns will emerge, helping you recognize your unique glimmers.

Cultivating Glimmers: Practical Strategies for Daily Integration

Once you've identified your glimmers, the next step is to weave them into your daily routine. Here are some practical strategies to help you get started:

First, create sensory-friendly spaces in your environment. For example, designate a corner of your home where you can retreat to enjoy your favorite textures, scents, or sounds. Keep items like soft blankets, essential oils, or noise-canceling headphones readily accessible.

Second, set aside time for glimmer activities each day. This doesn't need to be a long commitment—even five minutes can make a difference. Whether it's sipping tea in silence, listening to a favorite playlist, or cuddling with a pet, these moments can act as anchors in your day.

Finally, consider keeping a glimmer journal. Each evening, jot down one or two glimmers you experienced that day. This practice not only helps you stay mindful of these moments but also reinforces their positive impact on your well-being.

Case Studies: Real-Life Examples of Glimmer Integration

To illustrate the power of glimmers, let's look at some real-life examples.

Emily, an autistic woman in her 40s, struggled with chronic fatigue and sensory overload. She began incorporating glimmers into her morning routine by spending a few minutes feeling the texture of her favorite silk scarf and listening to calming music. Over time, these small practices helped her start her day with a sense of calm rather than dread.

Another example is Sara, a high-masking ADHD professional who often felt overwhelmed by her workload. She discovered that taking short breaks to watch her fish tank or enjoy a piece of dark chocolate provided micro-moments of joy that helped her reset and refocus.

These stories highlight the versatility of glimmers. Whether it's through touch, sound, taste, or sight, there are countless ways to integrate these moments into your life.

Overcoming Challenges: Common Pitfalls and How to Avoid Them

While glimmers can be transformative, incorporating them into your life isn't always easy. Sensory overload, lack of time, and self-doubt are common obstacles.

If sensory overload is an issue, start small. Choose glimmers that are subtle and non-intrusive, such as a soft fabric or a faint scent. Gradually build up your tolerance for sensory input as you become more comfortable.

For those with limited time, remember that glimmers don't need to be lengthy. Even brief moments can have a significant impact. Incorporate them into existing routines, like enjoying a calming scent while brushing your teeth or savoring a favorite texture during a work break.

Finally, if self-doubt creeps in, remind yourself that glimmers are for you. They don't need to be productive or impressive—they simply need to bring you joy or calm.

Moving from surviving to glimmers is a journey of self-discovery and self-compassion. By embracing these micro-moments of joy, you can begin to counteract the effects of neurodivergent burnout and create a life that feels more balanced and fulfilling.

Remember, glimmers are not a cure-all, but they are a powerful tool in your toolkit. They remind you that even in the midst of chaos, there are moments of light waiting to be noticed. Start small, be patient with yourself, and allow these tiny sparks of joy to guide you toward a brighter, more grounded future.

Take a moment right now to pause and notice something that brings you even a flicker of calm or happiness. That's your first glimmer. Let it be the beginning of a new way of being—one that honors your neurodivergent brain and helps you thrive in a high-demand world.

14

Building a Life That Accommodates Your Brain

For many high-masking neurodivergent women, life often feels like a relentless uphill climb. You've spent years adapting to societal expectations, pushing through exhaustion, and masking your true self to fit into a world that wasn't designed for your brain. Now, with a diagnosis or self-awareness of ADHD or Autism, you're ready to shift from surviving to thriving—but where do you start? This chapter is your guide to crafting a life that aligns with your unique neurology, one that reduces overwhelm, conserves energy, and allows you to reclaim joy.

Creating a Brain-Friendly Environment

The first step in building a sustainable life is designing an environment that supports your sensory and cognitive needs. For neurodivergent individuals, sensory overwhelm can be a daily challenge. Fluorescent lights, background noise, or even clutter can trigger stress and exhaustion. Understanding your sensory profile is key. Are you hypersensitive to sound? Easily overwhelmed by visual stimuli? Do you crave deep pressure or avoid certain textures? Once you identify your triggers, you can begin to make meaningful changes.

Consider replacing harsh overhead lighting with softer, adjustable lamps or natural light. Noise-canceling headphones or white noise machines can create a buffer against auditory overstimulation. Decluttering your space, even in small increments, can reduce visual chaos and create a sense of calm. For many, having a designated "regulation zone"—a safe space with sensory tools like weighted blankets, fidget toys, or calming scents—can be a game-changer. Remember, your environment doesn't have to look like anyone else's. It just needs to work for you.

Automating the Everyday

For neurodivergent brains, repetitive tasks can be energy vampires. Meal planning, cleaning, and scheduling often drain executive function, leaving little energy for the things that matter most. Automating these tasks can free up mental bandwidth and reduce daily stress.

Start by identifying the tasks that feel most burdensome. For example, if meal planning feels overwhelming, consider meal subscription services or batch cooking on weekends. Use visual aids like calendars, checklists, or color-coded systems to organize your day. Technology can also be a powerful ally—set reminders for appointments, automate bill payments, or use apps to track habits and routines. The goal isn't perfection; it's creating systems that minimize cognitive load and make life more manageable.

Setting Boundaries Without Apology

For high-masking women, setting boundaries can feel uncomfortable, especially if you've spent years prioritizing others' needs over your own. But boundaries are essential for protecting your energy and preventing burnout. Start by identifying your limits—what drains you? What brings you joy? Once you understand your needs, practice communicating them clearly and assertively.

In professional settings, this might mean saying no to additional responsibilities or requesting accommodations like flexible hours or remote work. In personal relationships, it could involve setting limits on social interactions or asking for support with household tasks. Remember, saying no isn't selfish—it's an act of self-preservation. Use simple, direct scripts like "I'm unable to take that on right now" or "I need some alone time to recharge." Over time, setting boundaries will become easier, and those around you will learn to respect your needs.

Real-Life Case Studies

To illustrate how these strategies can be implemented, let's look at two real-life examples. Sarah, a 35-year-old marketing manager with ADHD, struggled with chronic fatigue and overwhelm. After identifying her sensory triggers, she redesigned her workspace with dimmable lighting, noise-canceling headphones, and a clutter-free desk. She also automated repetitive tasks using scheduling apps and hired a virtual assistant for administrative work. Within months, Sarah noticed a significant improvement in her energy levels and focus.

Emma, a 42-year-old teacher with Autism, found herself constantly drained by social interactions and household chores. She began setting boundaries by limiting after-hours work emails and delegating cleaning tasks to her family. She also created a regulation zone in her home, complete with a weighted blanket and calming essential oils. These changes allowed Emma to reclaim her evenings and spend time on hobbies that brought her joy.

From Survival to Sensory Joy

Finally, it's time to move beyond survival mode and seek out moments of sensory joy. For neurodivergent individuals, these "glimmers"—micro-moments of pleasure and connection—can be deeply restorative. Start by identifying what brings you sensory comfort or delight. Is it the feel of soft fabric, the scent of lavender, or the sound of birdsong? Incorporate these experiences into your daily routine, even if only for a few moments.

Practice mindfulness exercises that engage your senses, like savoring a cup of tea or taking a walk in nature. Surround yourself with items that bring you comfort, whether it's a cozy blanket, a favorite scent, or a playlist of soothing music. These small acts of self-care can help you reconnect with your body and cultivate a sense of stability.

Building a life that accommodates your neurodivergent brain is a journey, not a destination. It requires self-awareness, experimentation, and a willingness to prioritize your needs. By creating a brain-friendly environment, automating everyday tasks, setting boundaries, and seeking out sensory joy, you can shift from merely surviving to thriving. Remember, your brain isn't broken—it's beautifully unique. Embrace it, honor it, and craft a life that allows you to shine as your authentic self.

15

The Role of Hormones in Neurodivergence

For many neurodivergent women, the journey toward understanding and managing ADHD and autism symptoms is often fraught with confusion and frustration. While societal expectations and masking behaviors play a significant role in amplifying these challenges, there's another critical factor that often goes unnoticed: hormones. Specifically, estrogen fluctuations can profoundly impact the neurodivergent brain, influencing everything from executive function to sensory processing. This chapter delves into the intricate relationship between hormones and neurodivergence, offering insights and strategies to help you navigate this complex terrain.

Estrogen and the Neurodivergent Brain

Estrogen is more than just a reproductive hormone; it plays a vital role in regulating neurotransmitters like dopamine and serotonin, which are essential for executive function, emotional regulation, and overall mental well-being. For neurodivergent women, estrogen's influence on these neurotransmitters can mean the difference between feeling grounded and experiencing heightened symptoms.

During phases of estrogen dominance, such as the follicular phase of the menstrual cycle, many women report improved focus, mood stability, and cognitive clarity. However, when estrogen levels drop—such as during the luteal phase, postpartum, or perimenopause—neurodivergent traits often become more pronounced. Sensory sensitivities may intensify, emotional regulation may falter, and executive dysfunction can feel insurmountable. This hormonal rollercoaster can exacerbate Autistic/ADHD Burnout, making it harder to manage the demands of daily life.

For example, Emma, a 35-year-old graphic designer diagnosed with ADHD, noticed that her ability to focus and meet deadlines fluctuated dramatically throughout her cycle. During the first two weeks, she felt energized and productive, but in the days leading up to her period, she struggled with brain fog, irritability, and sensory overload. Understanding this pattern allowed Emma to plan her workload accordingly, prioritizing tasks during her high-energy phases and allowing herself grace during the more challenging periods.

Perimenopause and Neurodivergence: A Perfect Storm

Perimenopause, the transitional phase leading up to menopause, can be particularly tumultuous for neurodivergent women. As estrogen levels decline, symptoms like brain fog, fatigue, and sensory sensitivities often worsen, creating a perfect storm of challenges. For many women, this phase can feel like their brain is betraying them, as they grapple with heightened symptoms on top of the physical and emotional changes associated with perimenopause.

Consider Sarah, a 48-year-old teacher with autism. As she entered perimenopause, Sarah noticed that her ability to manage sensory input—such as the chatter of her students or the fluorescent lights in her classroom—became increasingly difficult. She also struggled with memory lapses and fatigue, which made it harder to keep up with her teaching schedule. Like many women in her position, Sarah felt overlooked by the medical community, which often fails to recognize the intersection of neurodivergence and hormonal changes.

The lack of research and awareness around this issue means that many women are left to navigate perimenopause without adequate support. However, by understanding the connection between hormones and neurodivergence, women like Sarah can begin to advocate for themselves and seek out tailored strategies to manage their symptoms.

Hormonal Balance: A Path to Recovery

Achieving hormonal balance is a multi-faceted process that involves lifestyle adjustments, dietary changes, and, in some cases, supplementation. One of the first steps is to optimize gut health, as a healthy gut microbiome plays a crucial role in hormone regulation. Incorporating probiotic-rich foods like yogurt, kefir, and fermented vegetables can support gut health and, in turn, help stabilize hormone levels.

Reducing stress is another key component, as chronic stress can disrupt hormonal balance and exacerbate neurodivergent symptoms. Mindfulness practices such as meditation, yoga, and deep breathing can help regulate the stress response and promote a sense of calm. Additionally, certain supplements like magnesium and omega-3 fatty acids have been shown to support hormonal health and improve cognitive function.

Tracking your hormonal cycles can also provide valuable insights into how your body responds to fluctuations in estrogen. By keeping a journal or using a period-tracking app, you can identify patterns in symptom severity and plan your activities accordingly. For example, you might schedule high-demand tasks during phases of estrogen dominance and prioritize rest and self-care during times when your symptoms are more pronounced.

Building a Hormone-Friendly Lifestyle

Creating a lifestyle that accommodates hormonal fluctuations is essential for managing neurodivergent symptoms and preventing burnout. This involves listening to your body, setting boundaries, and prioritizing rest during high-symptom periods. For instance, if you know that your executive function tends to wane during certain phases of your cycle, you might delegate tasks or reschedule appointments to align with your energy levels.

It's also important to cultivate self-compassion and seek out community support. Many neurodivergent women find solace in connecting with others who share similar experiences, whether through online forums, support groups, or social media communities. Surrounding yourself with people who understand your challenges can provide a sense of validation and reduce feelings of isolation.

Finally, don't hesitate to advocate for your needs in personal and professional settings. If certain environments or demands exacerbate your symptoms, consider discussing accommodations with your employer or loved ones. Remember, your well-being is paramount, and prioritizing self-care is not a luxury—it's a necessity.

Understanding the role of hormones in neurodivergence is a crucial step toward reclaiming your mental and physical health. By recognizing how estrogen fluctuations impact your brain and body, you can develop strategies to manage your symptoms and navigate life's challenges with greater ease. Whether you're experiencing the highs and lows of your menstrual cycle or the tumultuous transition of perimenopause, know that you're not alone. With the right support and self-awareness, you can achieve hormonal balance and cultivate a life that honors your unique needs.

As you move forward, remember to approach this journey with patience and compassion. Reclaiming your neurodivergent brain in a high-demand world is no small feat, but by tuning into your body and prioritizing your well-being, you can create a foundation for lasting resilience and vitality.

16

Why Traditional Therapy Fails

For many neurodivergent individuals, particularly high-masking women with ADHD or Autism, traditional therapy often feels like trying to fit a square peg into a round hole. Cognitive Behavioral Therapy (CBT), the gold standard in mental health treatment, has been praised for its effectiveness in treating anxiety, depression, and other common mental health conditions. However, its emphasis on modifying thought patterns frequently falls short for neurodivergent individuals. This chapter explores why traditional therapeutic approaches often fail to address the unique needs of neurodivergent brains, particularly the sensory and neurological roots of their struggles. We will also delve into alternative therapeutic methods and provide actionable insights for advocating for your needs in therapy.

The Limitations of CBT for Neurodivergent Individuals

Cognitive Behavioral Therapy operates on the premise that changing negative thought patterns can improve emotional well-being and behavior. While this approach can be effective for many, it often overlooks the neurological and sensory realities of neurodivergent individuals. For instance, when a neurodivergent person experiences sensory overload in a crowded space, CBT might focus on reframing their thoughts about the situation rather than addressing the sensory overwhelm itself. This can feel dismissive or even gaslighting, as it implies that the problem lies solely in their perception rather than their brain's inherent wiring.

Research supports this critique. A 2020 study published in the Journal of Autism and Developmental Disorders found that CBT often fails to address the core challenges faced by Autistic individuals, such as sensory sensitivities and executive function differences. Participants reported feeling misunderstood and invalidated when therapists focused exclusively on cognitive restructuring rather than acknowledging their neurological realities. Case studies further illustrate this point. Sarah, a 35-year-old Autistic woman, described her frustration with CBT: "My therapist kept telling me to challenge my 'catastrophic thinking' about loud noises, but it wasn't just a thought—it physically hurt. I left feeling like my experiences weren't real."

This disconnect highlights a critical limitation: CBT's inability to address the sensory and neurological underpinnings of neurodivergent struggles. For neurodivergent individuals, particularly those experiencing burnout from years of masking, therapy must go beyond thought modification to address the root causes of their distress.

Misunderstanding Sensory Issues in Therapy

Sensory processing differences are a hallmark of neurodivergence, yet they are frequently misunderstood in traditional therapy settings. Many therapists, trained primarily in treating neurotypical clients, may misinterpret sensory overload as anxiety or emotional dysregulation. For example, a therapist unfamiliar with neurodivergence might attribute a client's aversion to fluorescent lights or tight clothing to "irrational fears" rather than recognizing these as legitimate sensory sensitivities.

This misalignment can exacerbate feelings of isolation and frustration. When sensory struggles are dismissed or misdiagnosed, individuals may internalize these experiences as personal failings rather than inherent aspects of their neurology. Emma, a 40-year-old woman with

ADHD, shared her experience: "My therapist told me I was 'overreacting' to the sound of the air conditioner. I felt so ashamed, like there was something wrong with me for not being able to tolerate it."

To communicate sensory experiences effectively in therapy, it is essential to find practitioners who understand neurodivergence. One practical strategy is to use sensory-specific language when describing your experiences. Instead of saying, "I feel anxious in crowded places," you might explain, "The noise and movement overwhelm my senses, making it hard to focus or stay grounded." This approach helps therapists recognize the sensory roots of your struggles rather than attributing them solely to emotional or cognitive factors.

Alternative Approaches to Therapy

Fortunately, alternative therapeutic methods are better suited to the neurodivergent brain. Occupational Therapy (OT) stands out as one of the most effective approaches, as it directly addresses sensory regulation and executive function challenges. OT practitioners work with individuals to develop strategies for managing sensory overload, improving daily functioning, and enhancing overall well-being. For example, an OT might introduce sensory tools like weighted blankets or noise-canceling headphones to help regulate sensory input.

Sensory Integration Therapy is another promising approach. This therapy focuses on helping individuals process and respond to sensory information more effectively. By creating a sensory-rich environment tailored to the individual's needs, practitioners can help clients develop coping mechanisms and build tolerance to sensory stimuli. Research has shown that Sensory Integration Therapy can significantly improve daily functioning and reduce sensory-related distress in neurodivergent individuals.

Neuroaffirming Therapy is a growing movement that prioritizes understanding and validating neurodivergent experiences. This approach emphasizes that neurodivergence is not a deficit but a different way of experiencing the world. Neuroaffirming therapists collaborate with clients to develop strategies that honor their unique strengths and challenges, fostering a sense of empowerment and self-acceptance.

Empowering Yourself in Therapy

Navigating the therapeutic landscape as a neurodivergent individual can feel daunting, but advocacy is key to finding the right support. Start by evaluating potential therapists using a checklist tailored to your needs. Questions to consider include: Are they familiar with neurodivergence? Do they prioritize sensory regulation? Are they open to alternative therapeutic approaches?

When discussing neurodivergence with a therapist, use clear, specific language to describe your experiences. Phrases like, "I experience sensory overload in environments with bright lights and loud noises," or, "I struggle with executive function tasks like organizing and prioritizing," can help convey the neurological roots of your challenges.

Finally, seek out practitioners who specialize in neurodivergence or have training in alternative therapies like OT or Neuroaffirming Therapy. Online directories and neurodivergent communities can be valuable resources for finding therapists who understand and respect your unique needs.

Traditional therapy, particularly CBT, often fails to meet the needs of neurodivergent individuals, especially those experiencing burnout from years of masking. By recognizing the limitations of conventional approaches and exploring alternative methods, you can find therapy that truly aligns with your neurological and sensory realities. Empowerment begins with understanding your unique needs and advocating for therapeutic support that honors your neurodivergent brain. In doing so, you take a crucial step toward reclaiming your well-being in a high-demand world.

17

The Lost Generation Boom

The past few years have witnessed a seismic shift in how society understands neurodivergence, particularly among women aged 28 to 50. This demographic, often referred to as the "Lost Generation," has experienced a staggering 400% increase in ADHD and Autism diagnoses since 2020. These women, many of whom have spent decades masking their true selves to meet societal expectations, are now facing a unique form of burnout—one that demands a radical rethinking of mental health strategies. This chapter delves into the statistical trends, demographic insights, and practical approaches that can help these women reclaim their lives and thrive in a world that has long misunderstood them.

The Statistical Tsunami: Understanding the Diagnosis Boom

The surge in adult ADHD and Autism diagnoses is nothing short of a statistical tsunami. Since 2020, the number of women seeking and receiving diagnoses has skyrocketed, driven by a confluence of factors. Social media platforms like TikTok and Instagram have played a pivotal role in raising awareness, with countless women finding validation in shared experiences that mirror their own struggles. These platforms have become a lifeline for those who have long felt invisible, offering a sense of community and understanding that was previously absent.

Another critical factor is the hormonal changes associated with perimenopause. For many women, these changes exacerbate neurodivergent symptoms, making it increasingly difficult to maintain the facade of "normalcy." Masking, the act of suppressing natural behaviors to fit societal norms, becomes nearly impossible when hormonal fluctuations amplify sensory sensitivities, executive dysfunction, and emotional regulation challenges. The result is a perfect storm that has led to an unprecedented rise in diagnoses.

Consider the story of Sarah, a 42-year-old marketing executive who received her Autism diagnosis last year. For decades, Sarah had managed to hold down a demanding job and raise two children, all while battling chronic fatigue and unexplained physical pain. It wasn't until she stumbled upon a TikTok video describing the experiences of high-masking Autistic women that she began to connect the dots. Her diagnosis was a revelation, but it also brought with it a profound sense of loss—for the years she spent masking her true self and the toll it took on her mental and physical health.

Demographic Insights: Who Are the High-Masking Women?

The women at the heart of this diagnosis boom share several common characteristics. They are typically aged 28 to 50, high achievers who have managed to navigate careers, families, and social obligations with apparent ease. Yet, beneath the surface, many are grappling with what they often describe as "mystery illnesses"—chronic fatigue, fibromyalgia-like symptoms, and a host of other conditions that defy easy diagnosis. These ailments are not mere coincidences; they are the physical manifestations of years of high-masking burnout.

High-masking burnout occurs when the brain loses its ability to process information due to the relentless suppression of natural behaviors. For neurodivergent women, this often means forcing themselves to engage in social situations, maintain rigid schedules, and meet societal expectations that are fundamentally at odds with their neurological wiring. The toll is immense, leading to a cascade of physical and mental health issues that traditional medical and therapeutic approaches often fail to address.

Traditional therapy, particularly Cognitive Behavioral Therapy (CBT), has proven to be particularly ill-suited for these women. CBT's focus on changing "negative thought patterns" can feel deeply gaslighting for those whose challenges are rooted in sensory and neurological differences rather than purely psychological ones. The frustration of being told to "think differently" about sensory overload or executive dysfunction is a common refrain among women who have tried and failed to find relief through standard therapeutic interventions.

The Roadblocks of Traditional Therapy

The limitations of traditional therapy for neurodivergent women cannot be overstated. CBT, which has long been the gold standard for treating anxiety and depression, often falls short when it comes to addressing the unique needs of those with ADHD or Autism. For women who have spent years masking their true selves, the suggestion that their struggles are merely the result of "negative thoughts" can feel dismissive and invalidating.

Take, for example, the experience of 38-year-old Emily, who spent years in CBT trying to manage her anxiety. Despite her best efforts, she found herself increasingly frustrated as her therapist encouraged her to challenge her "irrational beliefs" about social interactions. What Emily's therapist failed to recognize was that Emily's anxiety was not rooted in faulty thinking but in the sensory overwhelm that accompanied every social encounter. It wasn't until Emily sought out a therapist trained in sensory regulation techniques that she began to find relief.

Recent research has highlighted the need for alternative therapeutic approaches that focus on sensory regulation and neurological support. These approaches recognize that the challenges faced by neurodivergent women are not merely psychological but are deeply intertwined with their sensory and neurological realities. By addressing these underlying issues, therapists can provide more effective and compassionate care that truly meets the needs of their clients.

New Mental Health Strategies for Neurodivergent Burnout

For women experiencing high-masking burnout, the path to recovery begins with a fundamental shift in how they approach their mental health. Traditional burnout advice, such as "push through" or "socialize more," can be actively harmful for those whose brains are wired differently. Instead, the focus should be on sensory regulation, strategic unmasking, and lifestyle adjustments that accommodate their unique needs.

Sensory regulation techniques are a cornerstone of this approach. These can include the use of noise-canceling headphones, weighted blankets, and sensory-friendly environments that reduce the impact of sensory overload. Creating a "sensory diet" that includes regular breaks and activities that soothe the nervous system can also be incredibly beneficial.

Strategic unmasking involves gradually letting go of the behaviors and habits that have been used to conform to societal expectations. This process can be daunting, but it is essential for long-term recovery. Women are encouraged to identify the areas where masking is most draining and to explore ways to reduce its impact. This might mean setting boundaries with family and friends, seeking out neurodivergentfriendly workplaces, or simply allowing themselves to take up space in the world as they truly are.

Lifestyle adjustments are another key component of managing neurodivergent burnout. This can include creating a low-demand lifestyle that prioritizes rest and self-care, reducing unnecessary obligations, and communicating needs clearly to family and employers. Women are also encouraged to explore hobbies and activities that bring them joy and fulfillment, rather than those that are purely performative.

Case Studies: Real-Life Transformations

The journey to recovery is deeply personal, but hearing the stories of others can provide both hope and practical insights. Consider the case of 45-year-old Maria, who received her ADHD diagnosis after years of struggling with chronic fatigue and unexplained health issues. Maria's journey began with a deep dive into sensory regulation techniques, including the use of a weighted blanket and noise-canceling headphones. She also began to unmask in her personal life, setting boundaries with family members who had long expected her to be the "perfect" daughter and mother.

Over time, Maria noticed a significant improvement in her energy levels and overall well-being. She began to see her neurodivergence not as a burden but as a unique aspect of her identity that deserved to be celebrated. Maria's story is a testament to the power of tailored mental health strategies and the importance of honoring one's true self.

Another inspiring example is 37-year-old Lisa, who discovered she was Autistic after years of failed CBT sessions. Lisa's breakthrough came when she began working with a therapist who specialized in sensory regulation and neurological support. Through a combination of sensory regulation techniques and lifestyle adjustments, Lisa was able to manage her sensory sensitivities and reduce her overall stress levels. Today, she is an advocate for neurodivergent women, sharing her story to help others navigate the challenges of high-masking burnout.

The Lost Generation Boom represents a profound shift in how society understands neurodivergence, particularly among women who have spent years masking their true selves. The surge in ADHD and Autism diagnoses is a call to action—a reminder that traditional mental health strategies are often inadequate for those whose challenges are rooted in sensory and neurological differences. By embracing tailored approaches that focus on sensory regulation, strategic unmasking, and lifestyle adjustments, women in this demographic can begin to reclaim their lives and thrive in a world that has long misunderstood them. Their stories, like those of Sarah, Emily, Maria, and Lisa, offer hope and inspiration for a future where neurodivergence is not just accepted but celebrated.

18

The TikTok/Instagram Pipeline

In recent years, social media platforms like TikTok and Instagram have become unexpected hubs for neurodivergent communities. Terms like 'Autistic Burnout,' 'AuDHD,' and 'sensory overload' have entered mainstream discourse, offering validation and connection to many who had previously felt isolated in their struggles. For women diagnosed—or self-diagnosed—with ADHD and Autism in adulthood, these platforms have been both a lifeline and a labyrinth. They provide accessible information and foster a sense of belonging, but they also come with risks: oversimplification, misinformation, and the potential for overwhelm. This chapter explores the dual nature of social media as a tool for neurodivergent awareness and empowerment, while offering practical strategies to navigate its pitfalls effectively.

The Social Media Boom: Awareness or Overload?

The rise of neurodivergent content on platforms like TikTok and Instagram has been nothing short of transformative. For decades, adult women with ADHD and Autism were overlooked by medical professionals, often dismissed as 'overthinking,' 'too sensitive,' or 'just anxious.' Social media has democratized access to information, allowing individuals to share their experiences and educate others in ways that traditional healthcare systems have failed to do. This has been especially powerful for high-masking women—those who have spent their lives adapting to societal expectations, often at the cost of their mental and physical health.

Take Sarah, a 35-year-old marketing executive, who stumbled upon a TikTok video describing Autistic Burnout. For years, she had struggled with chronic fatigue, migraines, and a sense of disconnection, but her doctors attributed these symptoms to stress or depression. The video resonated so deeply that she began exploring ADHD and Autism further, eventually identifying patterns in her behavior and sensory sensitivities that had gone unnoticed for decades. "It was like someone handed me a map," she said. "I finally had words for what I'd been experiencing."

Yet, while social media can provide validation, it can also overwhelm. The sheer volume of content—often presented in quick, engaging snippets—can leave viewers feeling flooded with information but unsure of what to do next. Lisa, a 42-year-old teacher, described scrolling through hundreds of posts about ADHD, only to feel more confused. "It's like drinking from a firehose," she explained. "I'd get bits and pieces, but nothing cohesive or actionable." This is a common experience, and it underscores the need for discernment when engaging with social media content.

The Limits of 60-Second Clips: Why Viral Isn't Enough

The bite-sized format of social media has undeniable appeal. A 60-second video can introduce complex concepts like masking, sensory overload, or executive dysfunction in an accessible way. However, this brevity often comes at the cost of depth and nuance. For example, a TikTok creator might describe Autistic Burnout as 'feeling tired all the time,' but this oversimplifies a multifaceted neurological condition that involves years of suppressing natural behaviors and overwhelming sensory input.

Moreover, viral content can sometimes perpetuate misconceptions. One common example is the idea that 'everyone is a little bit Autistic.' While intended to reduce stigma, this statement erases the unique challenges faced by neurodivergent individuals and minimizes the need for systemic accommodations. Social media algorithms also tend to favor content that is relatable or entertaining, which can lead to the prioritization of certain narratives over others. A creator who jokes about forgetting their keys might get more engagement than one discussing the emotional toll of masking, even if the latter is more relevant to many viewers.

To navigate this, it's essential to approach social media content critically. Look for creators who cite reputable sources, share personal experiences without universalizing them, and acknowledge the complexity of neurodivergent identities. Bookmark posts that resonate with you, and take time to research these topics further through books, peer-reviewed articles, or professional consultations.

From Awareness to Action: Building a Personal Toolkit

While social media can spark self-awareness, translating these insights into actionable steps requires a more structured approach. Start by identifying the specific challenges you face—whether it's sensory overload, executive dysfunction, or chronic fatigue—and explore practical strategies tailored to your needs. For example, if you struggle with sensory sensitivities, experiment with noise-canceling headphones, weighted blankets, or dim lighting to create a more comfortable environment.

Unmasking safely is another crucial step. Many high-masking women have spent years suppressing their natural behaviors to fit societal expectations, and unmasking requires vulnerability and self-compassion. Begin by identifying small ways to honor your needs, like allowing yourself to stim in private or setting boundaries around social engagements. Sarah, the marketing executive, started by carving out 'no-meeting Wednesdays' at work to give herself a break from the sensory demands of back-to-back Zoom calls.

Creating a low-demand lifestyle is also key to recovering from burnout. This involves reevaluating your commitments and prioritizing rest and self-care. Lisa, the teacher, began by delegating household chores to her family and setting aside time for activities that brought her joy, like painting and journaling. "It's not about doing less," she explained. "It's about doing what truly matters to me."

Navigating the Community: Finding Support Without Burnout

Engaging with neurodivergent communities online can be incredibly validating, but it's important to approach these spaces mindfully. Social media can amplify feelings of inadequacy, especially when comparing your journey to curated posts or viral success stories. Remember that everyone's experience is unique, and there's no 'right' way to be neurodivergent.

Setting boundaries is essential to prevent burnout. Limit your screen time, unfollow accounts that trigger feelings of guilt or inadequacy, and take breaks when needed. Use social media as a supplement to—not a replacement for—professional support and self-reflection. Many women find value in joining smaller, more intimate groups where they can share their experiences and receive personalized advice.

Finally, recognize when it's time to step back. Social media is a tool, not a cure-all, and your wellbeing should always come first. As Sarah put it, "TikTok gave me the words, but it was up to me to write the story."

Social media has undeniably revolutionized the way we understand and discuss neurodivergence, offering validation and community to those who have long felt invisible. However, it's important to approach these platforms with discernment, recognizing their limitations and supplementing viral content with deeper exploration and professional guidance. By translating awareness into action and engaging with online communities mindfully, you can harness the power of social media to support your journey of self-discovery and recovery. Remember, you are more than a TikTok trend—you are a whole, complex individual deserving of understanding and care.

19

Practical Application: Real-World Strategies

Navigating life as a neurodivergent woman in a high-demand world often feels like walking through a minefield of sensory triggers, societal expectations, and internalized guilt. For those of us who have spent years masking our natural tendencies, the path to reclaiming our brains can feel daunting, especially when traditional advice falls short. This chapter is designed to meet you where you are, offering practical, actionable strategies to manage sensory overload, set boundaries, and avoid burnout. By the end, you'll have tools tailored to your unique sensory profile, along with the confidence to implement them in your daily life.

Mapping Your Sensory Profile: The First Step Toward Regulation

The foundation of managing neurodivergent burnout begins with understanding your sensory triggers. Sensory overload isn't just about loud noises or bright lights; it's a complex interplay of auditory, tactile, visual, vestibular, and even olfactory stimuli that can overwhelm your nervous system. Mapping your sensory profile is the first step toward creating a life that works for you, rather than against you.

Start by observing your reactions to different environments and stimuli throughout the day. For example, do fluorescent lights make you feel tense or fatigued? Does the hum of an air conditioner grate on your nerves? Are certain textures—like clothing tags or scratchy fabrics—unbearable? Keep a sensory journal for a week, noting any physical or emotional responses to these stimuli. This process isn't about judging yourself or labeling your reactions as "too sensitive"; it's about gathering data to understand your unique needs.

Once you've identified your triggers, prioritize them based on their impact. For example, if auditory overload leaves you completely drained, investing in noise-canceling headphones or earplugs might be a game-changer. If tactile sensitivities are a recurring issue, consider transitioning to softer, tag-free clothing or seeking out sensory-friendly fabrics. The goal is to create a sensory environment that supports your nervous system, rather than depleting it.

The 'No' Audit: Setting Boundaries Without Guilt

For high-masking neurodivergent women, saying "no" often feels like a betrayal of expectations—whether they're external (from family, friends, or colleagues) or internal (from your own perfectionist tendencies). However, learning to differentiate between tasks that are merely unpleasant and those that are neurologically harmful is crucial for preventing burnout. This is where the 'No' Audit comes in.

Begin by making a list of your daily responsibilities and commitments, both big and small. Next, categorize them into three groups: tasks that energize you (even if they're challenging), tasks that drain you but are manageable, and tasks that leave you feeling utterly depleted. The third category is where the 'No' Audit begins. These are the activities—whether it's hosting large gatherings, answering non-urgent work emails after hours, or attending social events—that your nervous system simply can't tolerate.

Setting boundaries around these tasks doesn't mean you're being selfish or lazy; it means you're prioritizing your neurological health. Start small. For example, if attending weekly family dinners leaves you overstimulated, consider suggesting a biweekly schedule or opting out of certain gatherings altogether. Communicate your needs clearly and without apology, framing them as self-care rather than rejection. Remember, your boundaries are valid, and honoring them is an act of self-preservation.

Case Studies: Lessons from Real-Life Unmasking

Sometimes, the most inspiring guidance comes from seeing how others have navigated similar challenges. Here are two case studies of high-masking neurodivergent women who successfully implemented sensory triage and unmasking strategies, offering relatable examples and actionable insights.

Case Study 1: Emily, a 35-year-old lawyer, struggled with chronic fatigue and migraines that she couldn't attribute to any specific cause. After mapping her sensory profile, she realized that the fluorescent lighting in her office was a major trigger. She invested in a desk lamp with warm, natural lighting and began wearing blue-light-blocking glasses. Emily also conducted a 'No' Audit, delegating tasks that drained her energy, like managing her team's social calendar, and setting boundaries around after-hours work. Within months, her migraines decreased significantly, and she felt more present in both her personal and professional life.

Case Study 2: Sarah, a 42-year-old mother of two, had always felt overwhelmed by the chaos of parenting. After identifying her auditory sensitivities, she introduced "quiet hours" in her household—times when noise was kept to a minimum, allowing her nervous system to reset. Sarah also made sensory accommodations for herself, like wearing noise-reducing earbuds during noisy activities and creating a calming sensory space in her home. These changes not only improved her well-being but also fostered a more peaceful environment for her family.

Avoiding Common Pitfalls: What Not to Do

While unmasking and implementing sensory regulation strategies can be transformative, it's important to approach the process with care to avoid common pitfalls. One mistake many neurodivergent women make is overcommitting to sensory regulation techniques, turning what should be a supportive tool into another source of stress. For example, while mindfulness meditation can be beneficial for some, it might feel overwhelming or inaccessible for others. The key is to find what works for you and let go of the pressure to adopt every strategy you encounter.

Another common pitfall is failing to account for environmental stressors that are beyond your control. For instance, you might create a sensory-friendly home environment but still struggle with overstimulation in public spaces. In these situations, focus on what you can control, like carrying sensory tools (e.g., noise-canceling headphones or a weighted lap pad) or planning quiet breaks throughout your day.

Finally, be mindful of the temptation to return to masking behaviors during times of stress or pressure. While it might feel easier to suppress your needs temporarily, doing so can lead to further burnout. Instead, remind yourself that unmasking is a long-term investment in your well-being, and it's okay to take small, incremental steps toward change.

Reclaiming your neurodivergent brain in a high-demand world isn't about overhauling your entire life overnight. It's about making small, intentional changes that honor your unique sensory needs and neurological realities. By mapping your sensory profile, setting boundaries without guilt, learning from others' experiences, and avoiding common pitfalls, you can create a life that supports rather than depletes you.

Remember, unmasking isn't a linear process—it's a journey of self-discovery and self-compassion. Celebrate each small victory along the way, whether it's saying "no" to an energy-draining commitment or finding a sensory tool that brings you comfort. You are worthy of a life that feels alive, authentic, and sustainable. This chapter is your roadmap to getting there.

20

Conclusion: A New Baseline

As we reach the end of this journey, it's important to pause and reflect on how far you've come. For many neurodivergent women, particularly those diagnosed in adulthood, the path to understanding oneself is often paved with confusion, exhaustion, and a deep sense of not quite fitting in. You've carried the weight of societal expectations, masked your true self to survive, and pushed through burnout until your body and mind could no longer bear it. But now, you're beginning to reclaim your neurodivergent brain—not as something to fix, but as something to celebrate.

This chapter is not just a summary; it's a call to action. It's an invitation to redefine your baseline, to move from merely surviving to truly thriving. Together, we'll revisit the key strategies that have been your lifeline, explore the psychological shifts that empower growth, and lay the groundwork for a sustainable, compassionate life that honors your unique neurology. This is your new baseline. Let's build it together.

Recap of Key Strategies

Throughout this book, we've explored a variety of strategies designed to help you manage your neurodivergent traits in a way that feels sustainable and healing. These strategies aren't quick fixes; they're tools to help you navigate the world with greater ease and authenticity.

One of the foundational concepts we've discussed is sensory regulation. Understanding your sensory profile is crucial. For instance, if you're hypersensitive to noise, wearing noise-canceling headphones in crowded spaces can be transformative. If bright lights overwhelm you, opting for dimmer lighting at home or wearing sunglasses indoors can provide relief. Sensory triage—prioritizing sensory needs based on urgency—allows you to address the most pressing discomforts first, creating a more manageable environment.

We've also delved into the low-dopamine detox, a practice designed to reset your brain's reward system by reducing overstimulation from activities like excessive screen time or social media scrolling. This isn't about deprivation; it's about creating space for healthier dopamine sources, such as engaging in hobbies or spending time in nature.

Another essential strategy is the 'No' audit—a process of evaluating where you're overcommitting and learning to say no without guilt. This practice helps protect your energy reserves, ensuring you have enough left for the activities and relationships that truly matter. These strategies, when combined, form a toolkit that empowers you to navigate daily life with greater intention and ease.

Moving from Surviving to Thriving

Surviving neurodivergence in a high-demand world often feels like an endless battle. You've learned to mask, adapt, and push through, but at what cost? The shift from surviving to thriving begins with recognizing that your needs are valid and that honoring them isn't selfish—it's essential.

One powerful way to cultivate this shift is by identifying and savoring 'glimmers.' These are the micro-moments of sensory joy that spark a sense of safety and contentment. They might be the warmth of sunlight on your skin, the soothing texture of a favorite blanket, or the aroma of freshly brewed coffee. By intentionally incorporating these glimmers into your daily routine, you create pockets of calm that counteract the chaos of the outside world.

Another crucial aspect of thriving is setting boundaries and communicating your needs effectively. This can be challenging, especially if you've spent years accommodating others at your own expense. Start small. Perhaps it's letting a loved one know that you need quiet time after work or politely declining an invitation when you're feeling overstimulated. Boundaries aren't walls; they're bridges to healthier, more balanced relationships.

Thriving also means embracing your neurodivergent traits as strengths rather than flaws. Your ability to hyperfocus, your attention to detail, your empathy—these are gifts that enrich your life and the lives of those around you. By reframing your perspective, you move from self-criticism to self-celebration.

Long-Term Sustainability and Self-Compassion

Sustainability is the cornerstone of your new baseline. It's not about finding temporary fixes but creating a lifestyle that supports your well-being over the long term. This requires ongoing self-care and a commitment to self-compassion.

One practical way to conserve energy is by automating routine tasks. For example, setting up automatic bill payments or meal prepping on Sundays can reduce decision fatigue and free up mental space for more meaningful activities. Simplifying your environment—decluttering your home or organizing your workspace—can also minimize sensory overwhelm and create a sense of calm.

Re-parenting your inner child is another powerful practice. Many neurodivergent women carry wounds from childhood, when their needs were misunderstood or dismissed. Re-parenting involves offering yourself the kindness, validation, and care you may not have received growing up. This might look like giving yourself permission to rest, speaking kindly to yourself during moments of struggle, or engaging in activities that bring you joy without guilt.

Self-compassion also means acknowledging that progress isn't linear. There will be days when you feel overwhelmed or revert to old coping mechanisms. On those days, remind yourself that healing is a journey, not a destination. Celebrate small victories and extend yourself the same grace you would offer a dear friend.

Building Your New Baseline

Your new baseline is a personalized standard of living that accommodates your neurodivergence. It's not about conforming to societal expectations but creating a life that aligns with your authentic self. This requires courage, creativity, and a willingness to advocate for your needs.

Start by identifying what truly matters to you. What brings you joy? What drains your energy? Use these insights to shape your daily routines, relationships, and goals. If you thrive in quiet, low-stimulation environments, structure your life accordingly. If you need more downtime than others, honor that without apology.

Celebrating your neurodivergence is a vital part of building your new baseline. Embrace your unique way of thinking, feeling, and experiencing the world. Advocate for accommodations in your workplace or social circles, whether it's requesting flexible hours, using assistive technology, or communicating your sensory needs.

Finally, remember that your new baseline is a living, evolving concept. As you grow and change, so too will your needs and priorities. Regularly check in with yourself, reassess what's working, and make adjustments as needed. This isn't a one-time process but an ongoing journey of self-discovery and empowerment.

Final Thoughts

As we conclude, I want to leave you with a message of hope and empowerment. Your neurodivergent brain is not a problem to be solved; it's a gift to be cherished. By embracing your unique traits, honoring your needs, and building a life that celebrates your authenticity, you're not just surviving—you're thriving.

The journey to your new baseline isn't always easy, but it's profoundly rewarding. Along the way, you'll discover moments of joy, resilience, and deep self-understanding. You'll learn to navigate the world on your own terms, finding beauty in the quirks that make you, you.

So, take a deep breath. Trust yourself. And step boldly into this new chapter of your life. You have everything you need to create a future that's not just sustainable, but radiantly, unapologetically you. Welcome to your new baseline. The best is yet to come.

www.ingramcontent.com/pod-product-compliance
Lightning Source LLC
LaVergne TN
LVHW100333210926
848480LV00003B/1327
* 9 7 8 1 9 1 4 2 7 2 6 6 0 *